SOCIAL LIFE
IN THE
DAYS OF PIERS PLOWMAN

SOCIAL LIFE
IN THE
DAYS OF PIERS PLOWMAN

BY

D. CHADWICK

NEW YORK / RUSSELL & RUSSELL

CAMBRIDGE STUDIES
IN
MEDIEVAL LIFE AND THOUGHT

FIRST PUBLISHED IN 1922
REISSUED, 1969, BY RUSSELL & RUSSELL
A DIVISION OF ATHENEUM PUBLISHERS, INC.
WITH PERMISSION OF CAMBRIDGE UNIVERSITY PRESS
L. C. CATALOG CARD NO: 73-77669
PRINTED IN THE UNITED STATES OF AMERICA

GENERAL PREFACE

THERE is only too much truth in the frequent complaint that history, as compared with the physical sciences, is neglected by the modern public. But historians have the remedy in their own hands; choosing problems of equal importance to those of the scientist, and treating them with equal accuracy, they will command equal attention. Those who insist that the proportion of accurately ascertainable facts is smaller in history, and therefore the room for speculation wider, do not thereby establish any essential distinction between truth-seeking in history and truth-seeking in chemistry. The historian, whatever be his subject, is as definitely bound as the chemist "to proclaim certainties as certain, falsehoods as false, and uncertainties as dubious." Those are the words, not of a modern scientist, but of the seventeenth century monk, Jean Mabillon; they sum up his literary profession of faith. Men will follow us in history as implicitly as they follow the chemist, if only we will form the chemist's habit of marking clearly where our facts end and our inferences begin. Then the public, so far from discouraging our speculations, will most heartily encourage them; for the most positive man of science is always grateful to anyone who, by putting forward a working theory, stimulates further discussion.

The present series, therefore, appeals directly to that craving for clearer facts which has been bred in these times of storm and stress. No care can save us altogether from error; but, for our own sake and the public's, we have elected to adopt a safeguard dictated by ordinary business common-sense. Whatever errors of fact are pointed out by reviewers or correspondents shall be publicly corrected with the least possible delay. After a year of publication, all copies shall be provided with such an erratum-slip without waiting for the chance of a second edition; and each fresh volume in this series shall contain a full list of the errata noted in its immediate predecessor. After the lapse of a year from the first publication of any volume, and at any time during the ensuing twelve months, any possessor of that volume who will send a stamped and addressed envelope to the Cambridge University Press, Fetter Lane, Fleet Street, London, E.C.4, shall receive, in due course, a free copy of the errata in that volume. Thus, with the help of our critics, we may reasonably hope to put forward these monographs as roughly representing the most accurate information obtainable under present conditions. Our facts being thus secured, the reader will judge our inferences on their own merits; and something will have been done to dissipate that cloud of suspicion which hangs over too many important chapters in the social and religious history of the Middle Ages.

G. G. C.

1 *January* 1922

AUTHOR'S PREFACE

THIS précis is intended primarily as a guide to the facts of social life recorded in *Piers Plowman* and is based on the three parallel versions of the poem as edited by Skeat. The wording, spelling and punctuation of quotations is that of one or other of these versions as printed in the edition of 1886, with the following slight alterations: *u* and *v*, *i* and *j* are sometimes interchanged for the benefit of the modern reader. When it has been found necessary to terminate the quotation before the next full-stop has been reached in the verse (as in the last quotation on page 32, printed in the text "flappes of scourges;") the full-stop has been added. Similarly if quotations ending with a full-stop are introduced into the middle of sentences the full-stop has been omitted (as on page 34, B xx 274). Very rarely a translation is substituted for a brief quotation as on page 11 ("keep the sanctuary"), or pages 8, 13 and possibly elsewhere.

Reference is made in the footnotes to the first line only of the passage on which statements in the Index are based; but the reader will recognise that the lines immediately following this first line are frequently most important, as on page 34, note 8.

As in Volume II of Skeat's edition a complete index is given to proper names, proverbs, parables and similes, it was necessary to include in this Index only those which were of special interest. A List of Bible References is given as a rough help to any who may wish to test and examine the numerous, and sometimes vague, references and quotations.

Though the statements in the Index depend on the three versions of the poem, a few other books, supplementary and confirming these, are referred to in the footnotes. The List of Authorities contains the full titles of such works.

D. CHADWICK

King's Lynn
18 *January* 1922

CONTENTS

LIST OF AUTHORITIES
MENTIONED IN THE FOOTNOTES

Ballad Book, ed. W. Allingham. London, 1913.

    26. Alison Gross.

    29. Robin Hood rescuing the Widow's Three Sons.

    32. Etin the Forester.

    40. A Lytell Geste of Robyn Hode.

    65. Lizie Lindsay.

    74. Glasgerion.

Blomefield and Parkin. *Essay towards a Topographical History of the County of Norfolk*, by F. Blomefield and C. Parkin. London, 1805–1810.

Bonaventura, St. *Life of St Francis*, translated by E. Gurney Salter. Everyman Edn. 1910.

Brunne, Robert of. *Handlyng Synne*, ed. F. J. Furnivall. E.E.T.S. 1901.

Cesarii Heisterbachensis *Dialogus Miraculorum*, ed. J. Strange. Cologne, 1851.

Chaucer. *Complete Works of Geoffrey Chaucer*, ed. W. W. Skeat. Oxford, 1894.

    Hous of Fame.

    Prologue to the Canterbury Tales.

Chester Plays, re-edited from the MSS. by H. Deimling. E.E.T.S. 1893, extra series, number xvii. Christ's Descent into Hell.

Coldingham Priory *Accounts* etc. Surtees Soc. 1841.

Creighton, C. *History of Epidemics in Britain*. Cambridge, 1891.

Cutts, E. L. *Scenes and Characters of the Middle Ages*. London, 1872.

Edward I, Wardrobe Account, ed. J. Topham. London, 1787.

English Historical Review, January, 1911.

Everyman with other Interludes, Everyman Edition; 1909.

    Everyman.

    The Chester Pageant of the Deluge.

    The Wakefield Second Shepherd's Play.

Felder, Hilarin. *Studien im Franziskanerorden*. Freiburg i/B, 1904.

Foxe, John. *Acts and Monuments*, ed. S. R. Catley. London, 1837.

Froissart, Sir John. *The Chronicles of Froissart*, translated by John Bourchier, Lord Berners, ed. G. C. Macaulay. London, 1913.

Glaber, Ralph. *Migne. P.L.* vol. 142.

Gower. *The Works of John Gower, Vox Clamantis*, ed. G. C. Macaulay. Oxford, 1899–1902.

Jusserand, J. J. *English Wayfaring Life in the Middle Ages*. New edition; London, 1920.

Langlois, Ch.-V. *La Vie en France au moyen âge d'après quelques moralistes du temps*. Paris, 1908.

La Tour Landry. *The Book of the Knight of La Tour Landry*, ed. T. Wright. E.E.T.S. 1868.

Liber Albus, volume I, ed. T. Riley. Rolls Series, 1859.

Mapes, Walter. *De Nugis Curialium*, ed. T. Wright. Camden Society, 1850.

Memorials of London, ed. T. Riley. London, 1868.

Mirror of Perfection, translated by R. Steele. Everyman Edn. 1910.

Myrc, John. *Instructions for Parish Priests*, ed. E. Peacock. E.E.T.S. 1868.

Owen, D. L. *Piers Plowman, a comparison with some earlier and contemporary French allegories*. London, 1912.

Paston Letters, ed. J. Gairdner. London, 1907; vol. I. of text.

Pecock, R. *The Repressor of Overmuch Blaming of the Clergy*, ed. C. Babington. Rolls Series, 1860.

Piers the Plowman, The Vision of William concerning, in three parallel texts together with *Richard the Redeless*, ed. W. W. Skeat. Oxford, 1886.

Piers Plowman's Crede, ed. T. Wright. 1883.

Political Poems and Songs relating to English History, composed during the period from the accession of Edw. III to that of Ric. III, ed. T. Wright. Rolls Series, 1859–1861.

    vol. I. 12. John of Bridlington.

            18. On the Earthquake of 1382.

            19. On the Council of London.

            20. Song against the Friars.

            22. On the Times 1388.

            24. On the Pestilence (1391).

SOCIAL LIFE
IN THE
DAYS OF PIERS PLOWMAN

ERRATA FOR

SOCIAL LIFE IN THE DAYS OF PIERS PLOWMAN

The main errata are on matters of coinage (pp. 69–70).

(a) There were no "copper" coins in England in the 14th (or 15th) centuries.

(b) The designs of "noble" and "groat" were not so exactly similar as the text might imply. The noble bears a king with sword and shield on a ship; the groat has a king's head crowned.

(c) "Groats" were first struck in the reign of Ed. III; it is therefore questionable whether they had become the "commonest" silver coins.

(d) "Pence" and "farthings" were of silver.

(e) There was no coined "shilling" until Henry VII's reign; until then, the "shilling" was only money of account.

p. 103. *For* "signing" of charters *read* "sealing." No signing was necessary until the Statute of Frauds. See B. II. 112, "this dede I assele."

p. 100. A reviewer in *The Manchester Guardian* has expressed strong disagreement with these generalizations on the medieval woman; and we are loth to neglect such criticisms from a serious source, even when they cannot be called corrections of fact. Both author and editor, on careful reconsideration, are still convinced that these words represent the actual documentary evidence; but their epigrammatic conciseness, necessitated by the whole plan of the book, may well have misled some readers. They would prefer now, therefore, to write thus:

"There was a very general tendency, *in ecclesiastical circles*, to a painful depreciation of women. Marriage (in spite of frequent protests that no such blame was intended) was often regarded by the clergy as a practical confession of failure, since the titles of 'virgin' and 'martyr' were most desirable. It will be remembered that Chaucer is even more explicit than Langland on the subject of clerical antifeminism; and if Chaucer, like Dante, gives us fine types of women, these owe far more to the troubadour tradition than to any ecclesiastical source."

INTRODUCTION

F EW other works give a better insight into English life and
thought in the fourteenth century than *Piers Plowman*.
The loosely connected allegory enabled the writer to attack
abuses he would not have dared to mention openly. Direct
satire of great persons in Church or State would have been
disastrous to him; but he could occasionally give mere personifications the characteristics and even the appearance of well-
known persons. In a more carefully planned work there would
have been no room for the vague allusions and the detailed
descriptions to which the allegory frequently gives place. It
was safest for Dame Study to attack the customs of degenerate
clerks and knights and for a visionary confessor, "coped as a
frere," to console Lady Mede. But frequently the personifications disappear; and pictures of ordinary men and women reveal,
more satisfactorily than many abstract arguments, the bishop's
lack of dignity, the pardoner's duplicity, and the labourer's inde-
pendence. Descriptions of miserable homes and beggar-haunted
highways expose the plight of lower orders of society in whom
Chaucer took no interest. Fashions and habits of all ranks of
society are preserved in the pictures of Lady Mede, the Field
Full of Folk, Beton's tavern.

An attempt has been made to collect and arrange under
definite headings the details given in *Piers Plowman* of fourteenth-century life and opinions. Where space permits, the
original words, from whichever version seemed most suitable,
are retained; but many interesting passages are too long to be
quoted in what is merely an index. Since the three versions
differ in many particulars, references are given to all three texts
and remarkable changes are noted. It is then obvious when
additions have been made or points omitted.

The account of society given in *Piers Plowman* is gloomy.
The writer obviously wished to expose corruptions rather than
to entertain his readers; and, in contemporary songs and
poems, the period "sitthe the pestilence" is not represented as

a golden age for England. But though, in despair, he once exclaimed

> God is def now a dayes · and deyneth nouht ous to huyre,

he did not give up all hope and looked forward to an age of peace. Then, as he says,

> Shal na more Mede · be maistre, as she is nouthe,
> Ac love and lowenesse · and lewte togederes,
> Thise shul be maistres on molde · treuthe to save.
>   And who-so trespasseth ayein treuthe · or taketh aȝein his wille,
> Leute shal don hym lawe · and no lyf elles.
> Shal no seriaunt for here servyse · were a silke howve,
> Ne no pelure in his cloke · for pledyng atte barre.
> Mede of mys-doeres · maketh many lordes,
> And over lordes lawes · reuleth the rewmes.
>   Ac kynde love shal come ȝit · and conscience togideres,
> And make of lawe a laborere · suche love shal arise,
> And such a pees amonge the peple · and a perfit trewthe,
> That Jewes shal wene in here witte · and waxen wonder glade,
> That Moises or Messie · be come in-to this erthe,
> And have wonder in here hertis · that men beth so trewe.
>   Alle that bereth baslarde · brode swerde or launce,
> Axe other hachet · or eny wepne ellis,
> Shal be demed to the deth · but if he do it smythye
> In-to sikul or to sithe · to schare or to kulter;
> Eche man to pleye with a plow · pykoys or spade,
> Spynne, or sprede donge · or spille hym-self with sleuthe.
>   Prestes and persones · with *placebo* to hunte,
> And dyngen upon David · eche a day til eve.
> Huntynge or haukynge · if any of hem use,
> His boste of his benefys · worth bynome hym after.
> Shal neither kynge ne knyȝte · constable ne meire
> Over-lede the comune · ne to the courte sompne,
> Ne put hem in panel · to don hem pliȝte here treuthe,
> But after the dede that is don · one dome shal rewarde,
> Mercy or no mercy · as treuthe wil acorde.
>   Kynges courte and comune courte · consistorie and chapitele,
> Al shal be but one courte · and one baroun be justice;
> Thanne worth Trewe-tonge, a tidy man · that tened me nevere.
> Batailles shal non be · ne no man bere wepne,
> And what smyth that ony smytheth · be smyte therwith to dethe.

No attempt has been made in this book to argue out the problem whether *Piers Plowman* is the work of one or of many writers. For practical purposes, however, it is necessary to proceed upon one assumption or the other; and the assumption here is that the three versions were written by one man. From the point of view of matter this seems very probable. Though many details are added in the succeeding versions, it will be noticed that there is seldom any actual change in attitude or argument. Such changes as do appear might be accounted for by the stiffening of a middle-aged man's opinions, or, in the case of references to contemporary events, by the lapse of time. It is noteworthy that, on the majority of subjects disputed by contemporaries, such as the Pope's power of pardoning sin, and the position of the labourer, the later versions do not contradict earlier views, but tend rather to amplify them. It seems hard to believe that in less than a century there should be three or more reformers, who differed so little in their ideals and their methods of expressing their views on contemporary society, that two or more of them were able and willing consistently to carry on the work of obviously original-minded predecessors.

If, however, the three versions are the work of many writers, the facts recorded and repeated in them are valuable as representing the accumulated experience of a group of men. Also, if this is the case, the figure of the dreamer will be interesting as a character peculiarly attractive at that period; for each writer has retained the previous suggestions of his character, even when adding fresh details. If, on the other hand, the dreamer is in all three versions the creation of one man, it is not unlikely that he shares the experiences of the author. Even the allusions to his name, appearance and disposition may be of autobiographical value. They are briefly stated below as though they were.

The dreamer is known throughout the three versions as "Wille[1]," or William[2], but neither his surname nor his birthplace is mentioned. He fell asleep "on a may morwenyng on Malverne hulles[3]" by the side of a stream, but he mentions the Malvern hills again[4] only to refer to the mists over them or his own destitution in that wild place. The only locality in which he says he lived is London. In the third version the line

Ich have lyved in London · meny longe ʒeres[5],

replaces the earlier version:

"I have lyved in londe," quod I · "my name is Longe Wille[6]."

1 A ix 118, xii 51, 89, 99, 103; B viii 124, xi 44; C ii 5, xi 71. 2 A v 44, cf. B v 62; C vii 2. 3 C i 6, cf. A p 5, B p 5. 4 A p 88, viii 130; B p 214, vii 141; C i 163, x 295. 5 C xvii 286. 6 B xv 148.

The writer is obviously familiar with life in the city; he refers
to a previous mayor by name[1], mentions the women of Flanders
who frequented certain quarters, and speaks of Westminster,
Cheapside, Tyburn, and Cock Lane[2]. The dreamer speaks of
a time[3]

> whanne ich wonede on Cornehulle,
> Kytte and ich in a cote · clothed as a lollere,
> And lytel y-lete by · leyve me for sothe,
> Among lollares of London · and lewede heremytes;
> For ich made of tho men · as reson me tauhte.

At another time he says that he was no more popular in higher
circles and was held as a fool because he was[4]

> loth to reverencen
> Lordes or ladyes · or any lyf elles,
> As persones in pellure · with pendauntes of sylver.

His height gained for him the name of "Longe Wille." He
says that he was unfitted for manual labour, since he was[5]

> to waik to worche · with sykel other with sythe,
> And to long. leyf me · lowe for to stoupe,
> To worchen as a workeman · eny whyle to dure.

And speaking of "A muche man[6]," he compares him with
himself. He was happiest when he was clad in "longe clothes[7]"
for he was a clerk, entitled to wear the tonsure[8].

> ich lyve in Londone · and on Londone bothe,
> The Jomes that ich laboure with · and lyflode deserve
> Ys *pater-noster* and my pryner · *placebo* and *dirige*,
> And my sauter som tyme · and my sevene psalmes[9].

But the life was a hard one and his happiest recollections[10]
were of the cloister to which he had been sent in his boyhood
by father and friends. As he seems to have accepted woollen
clothes[11] in payment for copying he did for the merchants, he
cannot have risen very high (which possibly accounts for his
lenient treatment of the poor clerks). His marriage[12] with Kitte
would hamper his career.

The idleness[13] to which he confessed was atoned for in later life.
He describes[14] how Repentance "made Wille to wepe · water

---

1 B XIII 271.   2 A II 131, V 129, 162; B II 160, V 319; C III 174,
VII 366 ff.   3 C VI I.   4 B XV 5.   5 C VI 23.   6 A IX 61;
B VIII 70; C XI 68.   7 C VI 41.   8 B XI 35; C XII 197.   9 C VI 44.
10 C VI 36. 11 A VIII 43. 12 C VIII 304. 13 C VI 93. 14 C VII 2, cf.
A V 44; B V 62.

with hus eyen," and describes elsewhere several of the penances
he performed; at one time he says he is walking about[1] "wolleward and wete-shoed," at another he calls " Kitte my wyf · and
Kalote my douȝter[2]" to perform the Good Friday penance with
him. Wille seems to have been little affected by idleness at the
time he beheld his visions, for he noc only liked verse-making[3]
but sought for information of all kinds of crafts[4]. His visions,
it is suggested, occurred at different times of his life, and the
intervals between these further complicate the three accounts.
After the vision of the Deadly Sins and Piers Plowman he
wandered about in his russet gown[5] in search of Do-well for a
whole summer before he encountered the two friars on a Friday.
Covetousness of the Eyes[6] was his companion for forty-five
winters; and it was only after a lapse of years[7] that he began
to fear the menaces of age which had been described in a previous vision[8].

Skeat, referring to the allusions to contemporary events, suggests that the poet began to write in 1362 when, about the age
of thirty, he produced the first part of the A-text. In 1377 he
probably began to expand his poem into the B-text, since, in
this, references occur to the last years of Edward III's reign.
The third version, in which Skeat reads a severe warning to
Richard II[9], would be written after 1392. Each of the two last
versions was certainly the work of a writer who, like the dreamer,
had taken more than an ordinary interest in his fellows, and
had lived in circumstances enabling him to acquire knowledge
of all kinds, from farmwork to Westminster law[10]. Even if the
events of the dreamer's life are purely imaginary, he is the
mouthpiece of a reformer who combined an enquiring spirit
with a prudent regard for time-honoured institutions and who
dared to record what most men attempted to suppress. Though
he sympathised with the hard-working mother in the hovel, he
protested against a system which broke down social barriers in
Church and State. If his own Utopia[11] were not to be realised,

---

1 B xviii 1, cf. C xxi 1.   2 B xviii 426, cf. C xxi 473.   3 B xii 16.
4 B xv 47; C xvii 209.   5 A ix 1; B viii 1; C xi 1.   6 B xi 46;
xii 3, cf. C xv 3.   7 B x 11 6; C xvi 6.   8 B xi 43; C xiii 1.
9 C iv 203–210.   10 See Skeat, Notes, Vol. ii. Cf. A ii 60; B ii 73,
xiii 427, xix 476; C iii 78, iv 190, viii 87, xxii 481.   11 B iii 297;
C iv 455.

he preferred the customs of the preceding age to those introduced since the pestilence. Frequently he seems to adopt the attitude of a man who, feeling the gradual decay of his own powers[1], laments contemporary unrest and decadence, and spares no class of society which derives material benefit from a corrupt system.

1 B xx 182; C xxiii 183.

I

SECULAR AND REGULAR CLERGY

SECULARS

THE splendid appearance of the prelates impressed the be-
holder with the majesty of the medieval Church[1]. Rich
robes and clean garments of fine gauze or cloth of Tartary,
anointed hair and shaven crown concealed beneath a cap, the
bishop's crosier "hoked on that one ende to halie men fro helle,"
and with "pyke...to pulte adown the wikked[2]," were symbolical of the Church's triumph over secular authority. The
primary significance of the dress and its accessories was over-
shadowed in the fourteenth century by its contemporary importance. Teachers of Christianity were honoured as representatives of an autocratic body long feared and obeyed. Keen eyes
such as those of Langland perceived, however, unmistakable
signs of decadence in the great organisation.

One of the disturbing symptoms[3] noticed by the poet was the
greed of lesser officials such as notaries and summoners.
Parishioners suffered from the prevalence of simony[4], since
rectors and parish priests were associated in the schemes for
acquiring wealth by fair means or foul. Either the evil grew
very rapidly or the poet's eyes, once opened, soon discovered
further developments[5]. The second version of *Piers Plowman*
contains more severe criticisms of the prelacy as a whole. The
poet denounces its members as hypocrites[6],

> enblaunched with *bele paroles* · and with *bele* clothes;

and warns them of Christ's wrath at the final consistory[7]:

> Lo, lo, lordes, lo · and ladies, taketh hede,
> Hit lasteth nat longe · that is lycour swete,
> As pees-coddes and pere-Jonettes · plomes and chiries!
> That lyghtliche launceth up · litel while dureth,
> And that that rathest rypeth · roteth most saunest.
> On fat londe and ful of donge · foulest wedes groweth;

1 B xv 222; C xvii 350.   **2** A ix 86; B viii 94; C xi 92.   **3** A ii 144;
B ii 166.   **4** A P 80; B P 83; C i 81.   **5** B xx 228; C xxiii 229.
6 B xv 113; C xvii 269.   **7** C xiii 219.

Right so for sothe · suche that ben bysshopes,
Erles and archedekenes · and other ryche clerkes,
That chaffaren as chapmen · and chiden bote thei wynne,
And haven the worlde at here wil · other wyse to lyve.
Right as weodes wexen · in wose and in donge,
So of rychesse upon richesse · arisen al vices.

The prelates desired other duties[1] than those of saving man-
kind by preaching and teaching[2], or of providing every Christian
with "bread and pottage[3]." The sainted Thomas à Becket[4], in
his proud contempt of secular monarchs, possibly set the standard
to which the finest type of fourteenth-century prelate aspired,
eager for personal distinction and fame. Less ambitious members
of the prelacy feared to face death, and "borel clerkes[5]" dared
to call their superiors "doumbe houndes."

Langland, like Wyclif[6], attributes the growth of this worldly
spirit to the Church's wealth. Undue accumulation of property
fostered pride and covetousness; during the first centuries[7] the
Church's possessions had been generously distributed, but in the
fourteenth century the prelates grasped the purse-strings tightly[8].
Not content with hoarding wealth which legitimately belonged
to the Church, ecclesiastics increased their resources by new
methods. Contemporary satirists remarked on the prevalence
of simony[9]; Langland[10] gives the impression that, from the Pope
and dignitaries of the Court of Arches down to the notaries and
summoners, he knew no official who did not profit by simony.
In order to supplement the stipend granted by the Church,
certain prelates held office under the Crown; the duties of
Church government being performed by subordinates[11]:

Bischopes and bachelers · bothe maistres and doctours,
That han cure under criste · and crounyng in tokne
And signe that thei sholden · shryven here paroschienes,
Prechen and prey for hem · and the pore fede,
Liggen in London · in lenten, an elles.
Somme serven the kyng · and his silver tellen,

1 C xi 196.   2 B x 267.   3 B ix 80.   4 B xv 551; C xviii 274.
5 B x 286.   6 Wyclif, edition Arnold, i 199, sermon lxiii.
7 B xv 239, cf. C xvii 363.   8 "Complaint of the Ploughman," Wright,
Political Poems, i 306, verses 7 and 8.   9 Wright, Political Poems, i 138,
"John of Bridlington's Prophecies," cap. iii, line 21; i, p. 356, "On the
Vices of the Different Orders of Society"; Wright, Political Songs, p. 323,
"On the Evil Times of Edward II."   10 B ii 62, xx 126; C iii 63, 127,
155, xxiii 127.   11 B p 87, cf. C i 85; Wyclif, iii 215, "Church
Temporalities"; iii 335, "Curs Expouned," cap. xxix.

> In cheker and in chancerye · chalengen his dettes
> Of wardes and wardmotes · weyves and streyves.
>   And some serven as servantz · lordes and ladyes,
>   And in stede of stuwardes · sytten and demen.

The tendency on the part of ecclesiastics to interest themselves ✓
in secular matters of national importance affected the Church's
position with regard to the great European nations. In addition
to spiritual qualifications her ruler soon required all the resources
of a secular monarch. The importance of the Pope's political
talents to the Church was illustrated by England's attitude to
religion during the fourteenth century. At the time of the great
schism England lent her support to the anti-French party.
Englishmen, barely tolerating the permission given to penitent
and provisor[1] to take English money from Dover, refused allegiance to a Pope who lived on French soil. A later remark shows
how strongly Langland and his fellow-countrymen disapproved
of the Papal Court at Avignon. A "curatour of holy kyrke"
reports[2]

> The comune *clamat cotidie* · eche a man to other,
> "The contre is the cursede⸴ · that cardynales come inne";

he gives as his own view[3]
>   I wolde
> That no cardynal come · amonge the comune peple,
> But in her holynesse · holden hem stille
> At Avynoun, amonge the Juwes ·
> Or in Rome, as here rule wole · the reliques to kepe.

Ecclesiastical interference in secular matters was less welcome
on account of the corrupt methods of Church government.
Wealth was said to be more powerful in Rome than in any other
centre of government[4]; and bribery was not unknown there.
Lady Mede, the personification of misused wealth[5], is represented by the poet as a welcome guest in the papal palace,
though

> Hue hath a-poisoned popes · hue apeireth holy churche[6].

---

1 A iv 116; B iv 133; C v 130. The toleration which the author here
affords to provisors (*i.e.* those who obtained presentations to benefices by
appeal to the Pope) is strange, especially in connection with C iii 182, iv
184, and the Statute of 38 Ed. III.   **2** B xix 414, cf. C xxii 418.
3 B xix 417; C xxii 421.   **4** A iii 208; B iii 214; C iv 272.
5 A ii 18; B ii 23; C iii 23.   **6** C iv 164, cf. A iii 123; B iii 127.

Langland[1] suggests that the system of appointing incumbents to the various sees and livings had degenerated into a scheme for increasing the Pope's power and his revenues. The word "pope-holy[2]" occurs in the poem; literally it meant "holy as the pope," but at this time it is used to mean hypocritical.

The poet's lack of confidence in the Pope appears in his remarks on pardons[3]. In obedience to his creed he acknowledged the Pope's power to pardon sinners; but he suggests[4] that a well-spent life is a surer passport to salvation than a bagful of indulgences or other pardons granted by the Pope. Later experience strengthened his conviction that, the less the Pope interfered in secular matters, the happier would be the state of Western Europe. The master-friar says

Al the witt of this worlde · and wiȝte mennes strengthe
Can nouȝt confourmen a pees · bytwene the pope and his enemys[5].

Men felt that reform must begin with

the pope formest,
That with moneye menteyneth men · to werren up-on cristine[6].

Even the clergy acknowledged that

Imparfit is the pope · that al the peuple sholde helpe,
And soudeth hem that sleeth · suche as he sholde save[7];

and laymen were unlikely to be desirous of supporting

the pope · that pileth holichurche,
And cleymeth by-fore the kyng · to beo kepere overe Cristyne,
And counteth noȝt thauh Cristene men · be culled and robbed,
And fyndeth folke to fighte · and Cristene blod to spille,
Aȝeyn the lawe bothe old and newe[8].

Such criticism of the Pope's conduct encouraged the belief that his spiritual power was limited and that pardon could only be granted to penitent sinners who tried to make restitution[9]. Thoughtful men had no faith in a parchment roll "with a peys of led·and two pollis amydde[10]"; they asserted[11] that not all the

---

1 A II 148, III 142, IV 116; B II 170, III 146, IV 133; C III 182, 186, IV 184, V 130; Skeat, *Piers Plowman*, II 38, 47.   2 B XIII 284; C VII 37. 3 A VIII 160; B VII 173; C X 324.   4 A VIII 156, 166, 173; B VII 171, 179, 186; C X 319, 330, 337.   5 B XIII 173, cf. C XVI 172.   6 C XVIII 233.   7 C XXII 430, cf. B XIX 426.   8 C XXII 444, cf. B XIX 439. 9 B XIX 181; C XXII 186; Wright, *Political Songs and Poems*, "Complaint of the Ploughman," pp. 306 ff.   10 B XIII 246.   11 B XVII 250; C XX 216; Wyclif, I 60, Sermon XXIV; III 362, "Church and Her Members"; III 459, "On the Twenty-five Articles."

pardons of Pampeluna and Rome could wipe out injury done to a fellow-Christian. The waferer, in return for service rendered to humanity[1], awaits from the Pope some material reward, such as a bull bestowing power to heal victims of the pestilence. He ironically accounts for the absence of miracles by the unworthiness of the people. Reverence for his creed preserved Langland's belief in the Pope's power to pardon[2]. His faith in the Church[3] held in check suspicions that imperfect cardinals could not create an all-powerful Pope.

There were few additions to be made in the final revision. The poet refers[4] briefly to the custom of trying in Rome cases in which wealthy persons were concerned; the best recommendation to the Pope's favour being wealth. "Poure gentil blod[5]" was denied honour in order that the rich man's son might "keep the sanctuary"—*i.e.* enjoy the privileges and emoluments of the higher clergy.

Langland's remarks on the Pope were not often doctrinal, but chiefly confined to criticism of the papal policy and claims; his knowledge of papal agents was more intimate. Superstition and the laxness of the parish priest prepared the way for the pardoner, as the vendor of papal indulgences was called. He obtained the bishop's sealed permission to visit parishes in his diocese, and made friends with the parish priest. He then took his stand in the church on Sunday[6] or in some public place, and offered pardon in exchange for money. In the "Field Full of Folk[7]"

> Ther prechede a pardoner · as he a prest were,
> And brou3t up a bulle · with bisschopes seles,
> And seide that him-self mihte · a-soylen hem alle
> Of falsnesse and fastinge · and of vouwes I-broken.
> The lewede men likede him wel · and leeveth his speche,
> And comen up knelynge · and cusseden his bulle;
> He bonchede hem with his brevet · and blered heore ei3en,
> And rauhte with his ragemon · ringes and broches.

In this way he impoverished the parish[8];

> the parisch prest and he · de-parte the selver,
> That have schulde the pore parisschens · 3if that heo ne weore.

---

1 B XIII 244; C XVI 219. **2** C I 138. **3** B P 108; C I 136. **4** C III 243. **5** C VI 78. **6** A II 197; B II 221; C III 231. **7** A P 65, cf. B P 68, C I 66. **8** A P 78, cf. B P 81; C I 79.

Other Papal legates shared the vanities of the lords and ladies they visited[1]; Langland[2] reproved them sternly for supporting liars, jesters and flatterers, and for denying alms to honest poor men. An ignorant incumbent appears, in the vision[3], enquiring for the four cardinal virtues. Hard experience has taught him[4] to shun the covetous cardinals who merely usurp that name[5]. When they last visited his parish, he and the poor clerks were obliged to provide lodging and fur robes for the cardinal and his dishonest servants, and food for their palfreys. He hopes that in future they will remain at the papal court at Avignon, competing with the Jewish money-lenders there in unholiness; or that they will keep guard over their relics in the churches at Rome. His protest against the privileges exercised by these prelates is echoed by the common people's cry[6],

The contre is the curseder · that cardynales come inne.

Prelates of distant dioceses followed the example of Pope and cardinals; and the English prelates were no exception to the rule. A solitary reference[7] to archbishops draws attention to their uncharitable dispositions. Though a bishop might lead the ideal life, "Do-best," and win a place amongst the apostles, yet there were few bishops who behaved charitably to good men, practising what they preached and reproving wicked men of noble birth[8].

In his first version[9] the poet states his opinion of the bishops' neglect of their duties, and charges them plainly with ignorance and corruption[10]. Through the neglect of the bishops, the much-coveted prebends had passed into the hands of undesirable candidates[11] who might in time rise to the prelacy. Endowments and benefices[12], founded in order that no priest need wander penniless from place to place[13], appear to have been granted by the bishop to undeserving persons.

When he revised his poem Langland saw further need for reform. The unity of Holy Church depended on the relations

---

1 B xix 446; C xxii 451.   **2** B xiii 422; C viii 82.   **3** B xix 411; C xxii 415.   **4** C xvii 365.   **5** B P 100; C i 128. See the characteristics of the cardinalate as described by Cutts in *Scenes and Characters*, p. 234. **6** B xix 415; C xxii 419.   **7** B xv 239.   **8** A viii 13; B vii 13; C x 13. **9** A iii 144; B iii 148; C iv 186.   **10** A ii 151; B ii 176.   **11** C vi 70. **12** A xi 192.   **13** A xi 197.

between the higher clergy and the laity[1]. For this reason he urged the many-titled bishop to continue to preach and teach and not restrict his energies to administering such sacraments as he was obliged to perform[2].

One considerable episcopal privilege is alluded to in the phrase "bishops' letters." The prelate had, from the Pope[3], a right of granting indulgences to worshippers at certain churches on certain occasions; and such indulgences had as full efficacy as if they had emanated directly from the Pope. Parishioners were also instructed to entrust unlawful earnings to the bishop, that he might secure salvation for them. Repentance taught[4]

> if thow wite nevere to whiche · ne whom to restitue,
> Bere it to the bisschop · and bidde hym of his grace,
> Bisette it hym-selve · as best is for thi soule.
> For he shal answere for the · at the heygh dome.

If the bishop would perform his duties to the layman, no interloper, such as the pardoner, would be able to deceive the parishioners. No "postele[5]" (as the "poor preachers" were called), or friar[6], had a right to preach or confess without his permission. But in the last version the poet complains that "lollers[7]" made their way into badly-governed dioceses and lived in luxury on honest men's earnings; "meny bisshopes" were like shepherds whose dogs were blind or dared not bark, so that the wolf preyed upon them at his will. Non-residence of bishops[8] had become a grievance; and possibly neglect of the duties of ordination was due in great measure to the bishop's absence from his diocese. There were priests who had

> noyther kunnynge ne kynne · but a croune one[9].

Bishops seem to have disregarded the necessary qualifications of knowledge[10], respectable birth and a proper "title," which would ensure that the priest, when ordained, should be able to live without making simoniacal bargains for his masses. There were bishops in the fourteenth century who preferred hunting and visiting rich landowners to performing their ecclesiastical duties[11]. The poet complains that steeds, hawks and hounds

---

1 B xx 317; C xxiii 319.   2 B xv 41, 449, 545, 561; C xvii 203, xviii 268, 283.   3 A viii 157; B vii 170; C x 320.   4 B v 297, cf. C vii 344.   5 B vi 151.   6 B xx 325; C xxiii 327.   7 C x 255. 8 B p 87; C i 85; Wyclif, iii 335, "The Grete Sentence of Curs Expouned," cap. xxix.   9 B xi 290, cf. C xiv 113.   10 B xi 303; C xiv 124. 11 B iv 124, cf. C v 120.

devoured money which should have clothed and fed the needy;
the beggar, because of his torn clothes, was driven away and
the "japer" (joculator) received silver[1].

Langland gives us another picture which destroys precon-
ceived ideas as to episcopal duties always being performed in
the Middle Ages with picturesque dignity. A curate had died
intestate. The bishop[2] entered his house to take possession and
spent a merry hour or two there with his men saying[3],

> he was a nygarde · that no good my3te aspare
> To frende ne to fremmed · the fende have his soule!
> For a wrecched hous he helde · al his lyf tyme;
> And that he spared and bispered · spene we in murthe.

This description of the bishop's visit was omitted from the
last version of the poem; but the poet's opinion of episcopal
conduct remained unchanged. He accuses mitred bishops[4] of
bargaining like brokers[5] and thriving on their ill-gotten gains
like merchants or even Lombard usurers. Money was made by
selling prebends and benefices to the highest bidder[6]. Avarice
barred their gates to the beggar[7]. Thus the prelates, who should
have reformed society[8], wasted their time and money in worldly
pursuits.

Abroad, charity was administered in the same spirit as at
home. Langland was never more wrathful than when he considered the Church's work in foreign lands[9]. Prelates took their
titles from Bethlehem, Babylon, Naphtali, Nineveh, Damascus
and Nazareth, but never visited their dioceses[10]. These bishops
in partibus remained in England, earning money by conse-
crating new altars and hearing confessions which should have
been made to the parish priest.

Of those who remained

> in Engelonde to huppe abowte · and halewen menne auters,
> And crepe in a-monge curatours · and confessen a-3en the lawe;

---

1 B ix 89.   **2** B xv 134.   **3** B xv 136.   **4** C v 193.   **5** C xiii 225.
6 C iv 32.   **7** C xvii 363.   **8** C xi 191.   **9** B xv 484;
C xviii 187.   **10** B xv 557; C xviii 279; Wyclif, i 282, Sermon lxxxiii.
When the holy places of Syria were lost to Western Christendom, a considerable number of bishops, planted in sees conquered by the Crusaders,
were cast upon the world. These were utilised as suffragans, or as bishops
with roving commissions; and the popes found them so useful in these
capacities that they perpetuated the practice. Such bishops *in partibus
infidelium* were usually friars.

the prelate bearing the title of Syria was specially advised to study and imitate the splendid example set by Thomas à Becket.

The task of enforcing the religious and moral code of Rome was deputed by the bishop to archdeacons[1], deans, and rural deans[2]. Langland notes that these officials shared the bishop's appreciation of a good bargain[3]. Sufficient money[4] closed the archdeacon's eyes to such sins as adultery and usury. The vices of rural deans[5] caused the poet to commend God's retributive justice which gave so great a share of men's unlawfully earned money to them, in company with "imparfit preests" and with harlots.

The power of these dignitaries was very great owing to the fact that one section of society lay out of reach of civil law. As long as the Pope was the supreme head of the Church, secular and regular clergy owed allegiance to him alone. By repeating the one verse of Scripture known as the "neck-verse," any offender could plead "benefit of clergy" and claim trial in ecclesiastical courts[6]:

Dominus pars hereditatis mee · ys a murye verset,
Hit hath ytake fro Tyborne · twenty stronge theeves.

Any criminal who could reach such a sanctuary as that at Westminster[7] claimed the Church's protection against civil authority. The laity wished that the Courts of King's Bench and Common Pleas[8] might be united into one Court with the Consistory and ruridecanal Chapter, so that there should be but one justice for the whole land. But Langland connects such aspirations with the Utopian hope that battles shall never again be[9];

For alle that bereth baselardes · bryght swerde, other launce,
Axe, other acchett · other eny kynne wepne,
Shal be demed to the deth · bote yf he do hit smythie
In-to sykel other into sithe · to shar other to culter.

The corruption of these ecclesiastical courts was well known[10]; bribery was commonly practised there[11] and the bishop's commissary protected all who rewarded him sufficiently. The poet

---

1 A P 92.　　**2** A II 150; B II 172, 173; C III 187.　　**3** C XIII 226.
4 B II 174.　　**5** B XV 128; C XVII 277.　　**6** C XV 129, cf. B XII 189.
7 B XX 282; C XXIII 284.　　**8** B III 318; C IV 476.　　**9** C IV 461, cf.
B III 303.　　**10** A III 137; B III 141; C IV 179.　　**11** A II 154;
B II 179; C III 190.

asserts[1] that silver alone ensured a speedy decision there. Evil reports were also spread of the part played by Courts of Consistory[2] in making and unmaking matrimony. The commissary of the archbishop of Canterbury's court, known as the Court of Arches[3], was ready to obtain a divorce for a patron who presented him with a valuable gift[4] such as a mantle of miniver[5]. Advocates and notaries decided appeals according to the presents they received[6].

The summoner[7] first announced the Church's intention of calling the evil-doer to account[8], and a sufficiently large bribe won from him a favourable report. His own short-comings[9] made him sympathise the more readily with other men's weaknesses. The poet[10] censures bishops for permitting the parishioners to depend for their peace of mind on writs of "supersedeas," issued through the summoners to stay proceedings.

In spite of the majesty of her prelates, Rome's greatest strength probably proceeded from her assertion[11]:

> There is no emperor king ne baron
> That of God hath commission
> As hath the least priest in the world being;

the power to administer the sacraments won for the priesthood the awe-inspired reverence of the people. Popular belief long continued to attribute special sanctity to them; though contemporary satirists made of the immorality of the clergy one of their stock jests[12], representing Sir Piers of "Prydie" in the inn with Purnel of Flanders by his side[13]. The eagerness of priests to obtain wealth caused Langland[14] to say that the covetousness of the friars had overtaken them. He is not hopeful for the

1 B xv 235; C xvii 362.   **2** B xv 236; Wright, *Political Songs*, "Satire on Consistory Courts," p. 155.   **3** B xx 137; C xxiii 138. **4** B ii 60; C iii 61.   **5** Though the word *divorce* is often used in this connection in the Middle Ages, it was regarded not as a separation of two parties once legally married, but as the dissolution of a matrimony which had never been valid. The commonest methods were to discover that the parties were within the prohibited degrees, or that one of the two had previously contracted betrothal or matrimony with some other person. **6** C iii 186.   **7** A ii 46, 147; B ii 58, 169; C iii 59, 187.   **8** A iii 129; B iii 133, iv 167; C iv 171, v 162.   **9** B xv 128; C xvii 277. **10** C iii 187, x 263.   **11** *Everyman*, Everyman edn, p. 20.   **12** A iii 145; B iii 149; C iv 187.   **13** A v 163; B v 321; C vii 367; John Myrc, *Instructions for Parish Priests*, lines 23 and 37.   **14** B xiii 11; Wyclif, 1 147, Sermon L.

clergy who take their duty of charity seriously[1]. Those who do so will have to beg their living, considering official clergy know so little of Charity of whom it is said

> Of rentes ne of ricchesse · ne reccheth he nevere[2].

The "prechers after selver[3]" were sometimes guilty of demanding payment for the sacraments[4]. The mass might be delayed until mass-pence were forthcoming; and food was asked in return for sermons. Priests[5], although they might be eager to point out the inferiority of the layman[6], often failed to set him a practical example of virtue[7].

Langland mentions[8] priests of a high type who put money to good use and expounded the Scriptures wisely, choosing such texts as "For you gladly suffer the foolish; whereas yourselves are wise[9]." He says that, owing to the efforts of such men, certain parts of the Bible had been translated for the benefit of the unlearned. He gives the impression, however, that they were in the minority; and it is probable that his vague allusion refers only to such scattered and fragmentary translations of the simpler parts of the Bible as one met with occasionally in our older literature, or merely to the preacher's habit of translating his text into the vulgar tongue before preaching on it[10].

God-fearing men began in the fourteenth century to question what were the duties and privileges of the priesthood. Langland preserves some of their opinions in his later versions. They held that priests were supposed to preach to, teach and help, all who needed material or spiritual aid[11]. A life-long example of purity and holiness was expected from the priest. He should be dead to the attractions of "spendyng-sylver[12]," since God provided him with food, wool, and linen.

> If prestes weren parfyt · thei wolde no sylver take
> For masses ne for matynes · nouȝte her mete of usureres,
> Ne neither kirtel ne cote · theigh they for colde shulde deye,
> And thei her devoir dede · as David seith in the sauter[13].

1 C xvii 335.   **2** B xv 172; C xvii 315.   **3** B xv 127; C xvii 276.
4 A iii 216, 237; B iii 222, 250; C iv 279, 313; Gower, *Vox Clamantis*, Liber iii, cap. 20, line 1561.   **5** A iii 128.   **6** A viii 117; B vii 130; Wyclif, "How the Office of Curates is ordained by God," *passim*.   **7** A iv 107, v 34; B iv 122, v 42; C vi 141.   **8** A ix 76; B viii 84; C xi 82.   **9** A ix 82; B viii 90; C xi 88. See Skeat, vol. ii.   **10** See Skeat's note on the passage.   **11** B xv 97; C xvii 251.   **12** B xi 278; C xiv 101.
13 B xi 274.

But the sad exclamation

> out of holicherche · alle yveles spredeth,
> There inparfyt presthod is · prechoures and techeres[1],

suggests that this ideal was seldom realised[2]. Langland constantly asserts[3] that, whereas a reformed priesthood might have saved the nation, the blind guides of his day led their followers to never-ending torment[4].

In the first revision attention is drawn to the unsuitable clothing worn by the worldly-minded clergy of the age[5]. The prescribed "peyre bedes" and breviary[6] were replaced by the baslard[7] (or short sword specially forbidden to priests) and by brooches. "Sir" John and "Sir" Geoffrey, as people entitled them, wore girdles of silver with a baselard, or a large knife known as a "ballok-knyf," adorned on the handle by gilt studs[8]:

> Sire Iohan and sire Geffray · hath a gerdel of sylver,
> A basellarde, or a ballokknyf · with botones overgylte.
> Ac a portous that shulde be his plow · *placebo* to segge,
> Hadde he nevre servyse to save sylver ther-to · seith it with yvel wille!

Some priests exchanged their clerical garb for the knight's "paltock[9]," or jacket, and fashionable peaked shoes. The dreamer was remarkable for showing no respect to parsons with fur robes and chains of silver[10].

Less successful priests who could not attain to this display seem to have gone to the other extreme, both in manners and appearance. A priest of evil mien[11], hailing from the marches of Ireland, appears in a vision:

> "By Marie," quod a mansed preste · of the marche of Yrlonde,
> "I counte namore Conscience · bi so I cacche sylver,
> Than I do to drynke · a drauȝte of good ale!"
> And so seide sexty · of the same contreye;
> And shoten aȝein with shotte · many a shef of othes;
> And brode hoked arwes · Goddes herte, and his nayles,
> And hadden almost Unyte · and holynesse adowne.

1 B xv 92, cf. C xvii 245.   **2** B xv 97; C xvii 251.   **3** B xv 530; C xviii 250.   **4** B xiii 13; C xvi 16; Wyclif, "How the Office of Curates is ordained by God," chap. iii, IIIrd default of Evil Curates. **5** Myrc, *Instructions for Parish Priests*, ll. 43 and 48; "Complaint of the Ploughman," ed. Wright, i, pp. 307, 331; Wright, *Political Songs*, p. 328, "On Evil Times of Edward II."   **6** B xv 118.   **7** The clergy even left these forbidden weapons by will; *e.g. Bp. Stafford's Register* (ed. Hingeston-Randolph), pp. 398, 413, in the years 1411–1415.   **8** B xv 120. **9** B xx 218; C xxiii 219.   **10** B xv 7.   **11** B xx 220, cf. C xxiii 221; *Rotuli Parl.* Index, p. 156 *a*; vol. iv, pp. 190 *b*, 254 *b*.

In the last two versions the poet shows the results of neglecting to exercise great care when choosing candidates for ordination[1]. Mass, mattins and hours were not celebrated with true devotion by men who could not read correctly[2]. There were some priests who habitually omitted portions of the service in their haste and were known as "over-skippers[3]."

From one passage[4] in the first revision Skeat conjectures that Langland thought the secular clergy should be allowed to marry. "Every maner seculer" might well in an ordinary context have been intended to include them as well as the laity. But here we can scarcely assume the poet to have believed that suitable marriages would prove the best remedy for the prevalent immorality, which led the clergy to spend Church funds "on aparail and on Purnele[5]" (a lady of doubtful reputation). The reference would probably have been far clearer if he had meant to hint at a solution which very few of his orthodox contemporaries would have allowed.

In his last version the poet exerted himself still further to win back the priests to love of charity, humility[6] and poverty[7]. He mentions their methods of extorting money from credulous laymen. The prelates and priests attributed to the images and relics in their churches miraculous powers, and, Langland says, they "soffren men do sacrifice and worshepen maumettes[8]." This form of "ydolatrie[9]," as he termed the false miracles favoured by the clergy for the sake of money, provided the guardians of the shrines with offerings of wax tapers and wax figures of sick persons seeking relief[10].

According to fourteenth-century literature, the parish priests were, with one exception, the most ignorant and least enterprising members of their order[11]. The frequency of non-residence probably lowered the standard and robbed the poorer parishes of many capable priests; the poet says[12] that after the pestilence parsons and parish priests, complaining of the poverty of their parishes, sought licenses from their bishops to sing in London

---

1 B P 97; C I 125.　　2 C XIV 121.　　3 C XIV 123.　　4 B IX 177; C XI 284. See Skeat, vol. II, note.　　5 C XVIII 71.　　6 C XI 196. 7 C XIV 100.　　8 C I 119.　　9 C I 96; Ralph Glaber, *Migne, P.L.* 142, col. 674.　　10 *Paston Letters*, ed. Gairdner, Text I 48.　　11 B XII 184; C XV 124; Chaucer, *Prologue*, l. 477.　　12 A P 80; B P 83; C I 81; Wyclif, "How the Office of Curates is ordained by God," defaults 10 and 21.

"for symonye · for selver ys swete." Appropriation and non-residence were unlikely to benefit the parish[1]. Either services were not held at all, or a substitute for the incumbent was sought from amongst the less competent or less influential clergy[2].

The rivalry of the friars is referred to in the first revision[3]; and their success[4] is sufficiently though indirectly explained by the confession of Sloth, "prest and person · passyng therty wintere[5]." The easy-going parish clergy were no match for the busy friars, who met with a good reception amongst the parishioners.

A great deal of knowledge was not necessary for a parish priest[6], since his pater-noster was supposed to serve him in place of learning or argument. Sloth, speaking as a parson, confessed that he could not chant, sing nor read the life of any saint[7]. He preferred the task of finding a hare in a large field to construing for his parishioners one clause of the well-known psalms "Beatus vir" or "Beati omnes." This ignorance was due to idleness rather than to stupidity; for a parson who knew nothing of the canon of the Mass or the Decretals, and could not translate Cato nor read as became a clerk, could yet conduct a "love-day" and receive the reeve's accounts. Hunting and hawking probably occasioned considerable neglect of duty; for Langland wished to punish indulgence in these sports by loss of benefice or even of life[8].

The chaplains who assisted vicars and rectors are said to have been frequently ignorant, avaricious and over-anxious to seize the offerings of charity[9]. The poet remarks on the lack of charity in their conduct to their kinsmen and all other Christians.

Such being the case, it was little wonder that Langland feared the influence of the clergy on the laity. In the first revision of his poem he declares that the "curatours," chosen to care for the people, had long forgotten their promise to preach and die for Christ's "dere children[10]." They were like the builders of Noah's Ark, for though they had established the Church as a refuge for laymen, they had neglected to protect themselves[11].

---

1 B x 313; C vi 165.   2 B xv 478.   3 B xx 282; C xxiii 284.
4 B v 143, cf. C vii 120.   5 B v 422; C viii 30.   6 B x 467.
7 B v 423; C viii 31 ff.   8 B iii 312; C iv 470.   9 A i 169;
B i 188, xi 306; C ii 187, xiv 127.   10 B xx 278; C xviii 293, xxiii 280.
11 B x 409; C xii 248.

Many clerks never attained to the priesthood. The writer of *Piers Plowman*, probably himself a clerk in lower orders, showed great interest in these less fortunate ecclesiastics and was inclined to excuse their shortcomings by a sympathetic account of the hardships they endured. When he revised his work he did not comment bitterly on them, as he did on the higher clergy.

The title of clerk was naturally attributed to all men of any learning in the Middle Ages, since university students, and often even schoolboys, were in lower ecclesiastical orders. Langland alludes to Aristotle as the "grete clerke[1]"; and prelates, including the pope, were "clerks of Holy Church" when their learning was emphasised[2]. At one time, he thought, decent birth had been a condition of admission to the lowest ecclesiastical order[3], which enjoyed the privileges of education[4], exemption from manual labour[5], and the right of being tried for all offences in ecclesiastical courts[6].

> Wel may the barn blesse · that hym to book sette;
> That lyvynge after lettrure · savede hym lyf and soule[7]!

Langland regretted that in his time the old barriers were broken down; and he dated national decadence from a time when, amongst other evils,

> bondemenne barnes · han be mad bisshopes,
> And barnes bastardes · han ben archidekenes[8].

Many a clerk aspired to nothing more than a humble living; but even there he was frequently disappointed, as Langland realised in later life. After acquiring sufficient knowledge to read Holy Writ and distinguish what was best for body and soul[9], he might possibly be obliged to earn a precarious livelihood by casual clerical work[10]. Such clerks frequented London and sàng funeral services; the surviving relatives paid them with a few pence or a meal in the kitchen. The dreamer describes this as his lot:

> ich synge for hure soules · of suche as me helpen,
> And tho that fynden me my fode · vouchen saf, ich trowe,
> To be welcome whanne ich come · other-whyle in a monthe,
> Now with hym and now with hure · and thus-gate ich begge
> With-oute bagge other botel · bote my wombe one[11].

1 B xii 266. 2 B xv 80, 102, cf. C xvii 255, xviii 68. 3 C vi 63.
4 B iii 343, xiii 293; C vii 42. 5 C vi 56. 6 B xii 189; C xv 129.
7 C xv 127, cf. B xii 187. 8 C vi 70. 9 C vi 38. 10 C vi 45.
11 C vi 48.

These clerks swelled the throng at funerals and helped with festival services such as that held on Corpus Christi day[1]. When everything else failed the clerk wandered from place to place, "wolleward and wet-shoed[2]," begging his food, and (except for his tonsure) indistinguishable from the vagabonds who also wore russet-coloured copes[3]. Ill-fortune reduced him to despair and idleness[4].

A certain number of clerks, on account of their superior education, found employment in the service of secular lords or merchants, and interpreted Latin and kept accounts[5]. Langland gives an instance of the kind of work they did, and the payment they received:

> Thenne were marchaundes murie · thei wopen for joye,
> And ჳeeven Wille for his writynge · wollene clothes;
> For he copiede thus heore cause · thei couden him gret thonk[6].

Clerks who had risen to the prelacy were admitted to the King's Council[7].

In spite of the poverty of these lower clergy, Langland could not assert their immunity from the vices of prelates[8]. English clerks were covetous[9]. They longed for groats and nobles to waste in luxury, and worshipped Lady Mede as faithfully as any bishop. They overwhelmed rich men with attention[10], though they neglected the poor. The contrast[11] between the professions of learned men and their evil practices inspired a comparison between clerks and false coins bearing the king's stamp in inferior metal[12]. Learning fell into disrepute, since, in noble households, the ignorant servants performed their duties better than educated men and sinned less grievously than the clerks of Holy Church[13]. Certain medieval arguments are repeated in *Piers Plowman*, warning men against the folly of trusting to learning, rather than to Christian virtues, for salvation[14]. According to tradition the great wisdom of Solomon and Trajan

---

1 B xv 381; C xviii 120; Blomefield's *Norfolk*, ix 202 (Robert Chambers' Will). 2 B xviii 1, cf. C xxi 1; Villon, *Petit Testament*, xxvii, xxviii; Walter Mapes, *De Nugis Curialium*, Distinc. i, cap. xxxi; Camden Society, p. 65, l. 18. 3 A ix 1; B viii 1; C vi 2, 56, x 210, 247, xi 1. 4 C x 205. 5 B iii 343, xix 459; C xxii 464. 6 A viii 42. 7 A iii 110, iv 152; B p 114, 116, iii 114, iv 189; C i 141, iv 151. 8 A iii 27; B iii 26, xv 513; C iv 27, xviii 214. 9 B xv 407; C xviii 208. 10 B xv 325. 11 A xi 56; B x 69; C xii 52. 12 C xviii 72. 13 B x 470; C xii 297. 14 B xiii 133, 201; C xvi 180.

and other wise men had not saved them[1]; Solomon[2] is said to be in hell and Trajan owed his salvation to love not to learning[3]. Christ had not commended learning, and had chosen homely folk rather than learned men[4].

Common sense prevented the poet from advocating ignorance. In spite of all their faults, the clerks were guardians of a precious treasure[5]; and pagan writings were considered too valuable to be neglected. Pious clergymen recommended the philosophers to the mercy of God and advised students to receive their words with caution[6]. It would be foolish, they argued, to follow the example of men who are now atoning in hell for their sins; but such wisdom as Aristotle's could not be despised. "Clergy," as learning was called, was valued also for the tools, such as compass and square, with which it provided craftsmen[7].

Churchmen were anxious to prevent learning from degenerating into the weapon of ambitious men. Serious men held that there could be no true science without religion and morality[8]; "clergy[9]" was accessible only to those who had been baptized and had passed by the pass of "Suffre-bothe-wele-and-moche-wo[10]"; and ridden past "Richesse," since

Yf thow coveite to be riche · to Cleregie comst thow nevere.

Long study alone achieved the coveted titles of "doctor" and "master[11]." Only the keenest students were likely to persevere in a pursuit which promised little worldly success or fame[12]. The encouragement offered was a promise of greater insight, and ability to use the help provided by the Church[13]. The fate of Lucifer warned the successful student of the reward of ambition[14]. The typical medieval student was lean and of downcast countenance[15]. His paradise was the school (a term which includes also the university) at which friends or parents supported him[16]. There he found "love and lownesse and lykyng to

---

1 B xii 266; C xv 190. 2 B x 395. 3 B xi 135, 160; C xiii 74.
4 A xi 286; B x 442; C xii 276, xxi 408. 5 B xii 111; C xv 54.
6 A xi 268; B x 387; C xii 221. 7 A xi 133; B x 177; C xii 125.
8 A xi 17; B x 17, xi 166; C xii 14, xiii 93. 9 A xii 14. 10 A xi 113; B x 157; C xii 107. 11 B xi 168, xiii 25, xv 373; C xvi 30, xviii 113. 12 A xi 13; B x 13; C xii 11. 13 B xii 172; C xv 111.
14 B xv 51; C xvii 213. 15 A xi 2; B x 2, cf. C xii 2; Chaucer, *Prologue*, l. 289. 16 B x 304; C vi 36, 156.

lerne..." and "bokes to rede." The unwilling pupil was despised and his studies were stimulated by the birch[1].

The poet mentions theology as a bewildering and dangerous subject, likely to lead astray the student whose faith was weak[2]. The uncompromising methods of the instructors[3], as suggested by the personification of Scripture, were hardly calculated to encourage timid students[4]. Of other branches of study, the "Seven Arts" were most revered[5]; and they provided work for many years. These were divided into the Trivium and Quadrivium. Boys were first thoroughly grounded in *grammar*[6], which meant a good deal more than it means in the ordinary parlance of our day; grammar-school education included, not only reading and parsing, but also construing and writing Latin. Then in his first year at the university the student completed the "Trivium" by studying *rhetoric* and *logic*[7], which Langland thought of little use without true belief. The "Quadrivium" consisted of *arithmetic*[8], a gift of grace, *music*[9] (or the study of "mensurable music"), *geometry*[10] and the difficult art of *astronomy*[11], taught by grace and dependent on the spiritual condition of society in so far as this influenced physical phenomena.

Latin was the learned tongue[12]. Though once in the poem the commons cry "in vers of latin" to the king's council "*Precepta Regis sunt nobis vincula legis*[13]," they are not supposed to have understood the address delivered to them in Latin. They only knew as much as was good for them to know.

French still seems to have been the language of polite society. Langland[14] connects "Frenchmen" with "freemen" as though (at the time of his first revision) the upper classes habitually spoke French and taught their children such proverbs as:

> Bele vertue est soffrance · mal dire est petyt veniance,
> Bien dire et bien soffrir · fait lui soffrant a bien venir[15].

---

1 A x 84, xi 132; B x 176; C xii 124.   **2** A xi 136; B x 180, xii 216; C xii 129, xv 156; see Layman's Religion.   **3** B xi 1; C xii 163. **4** A xii 34; B xi 103; C xiii 40.   **5** A xi 106; B x 150, xi 166; C xii 98, xiii 93.   **6** B xv 365; C xviii 107; Skeat, ii 152. **7** A xi 127; B x 171, xi 214; C xii 119.   **8** B xix 234; C xxii 240. **9** A xi 128; B x 172; C xii 120.   **10** A xi 153; B x 208. **11** A xi 152; B x 207, xv 352, 363, xix 238; C xviii 96, 105, xxii 244. **12** B i 139, xi 208; C ii 140.   **13** B p 143; Skeat's *Note*.   **14** B xi 375. **15** B xi 376, cf. C xiv 205.

Ignorance of French would only be confessed by an uneducated trader whose excuse might be

> I lerned nevere rede on boke,
> And I can no Frenche in feith[1].

But the use of French was becoming less usual; amongst the "new clerks" we hear that there is

> nou3t on amonge an hundreth · that an auctour can construe,
> Ne rede a lettre in any langage · but in Latyn or in Englissh[2].

A few French words and phrases occur in *Piers Plowman*; a hospital is a "meson-dieux[3]," Jacob addresses Joseph as "Beau fitz[4]," and a reproach is levelled against prelates who shelter behind "bele paroles" and "bele clothes[5]." We are told that

> Beaute saunz bounte · blessed was hit nevere,
> Ne kynde saunz cortesie · in no contreye preysed[6].

In one proverb Latin and French are curiously combined:

> Qant *oportet* vyent en place · yl ny ad que *pati*[7].

Though the independent labourers are said to require their food to be served "chaud" and "pluschaud[8]," and idle dykers and their companions sing the refrain "Deu vous saue, dam Emme[9]!" it is most probable that the labouring classes knew as little of French or Latin as of the "Englisch of oure eldres of olde menne techynge[10]." Their prejudices probably inspired the description of the devil as a "proud prikere" (or horseman) of France[11]. Minstrels called for "a largesse[12]" from their patrons at the high table, but Haukyn, the waferer, requests that he may be addressed in English: "I can nou3t construe al this"..."3e moste kenne me this on Englisch[13]." In works addressed to "Englisshmen...that mowen speke and huyre[14]," it was necessary to translate or comment upon quotations in other languages.

It seems from Langland's account that

> Doctours of decree · and of dyvyn maystres[15]

---

1 B v 239.   2 B xv 368.   3 A viii 28; B vii 26; C x 30.   4 A viii 148; B vii 162; C x 311.   5 B xv 113; C xvii 269.   6 C xviii 163. 7 B x 439.   8 A vii 299; B vi 313; C ix 335.   9 A p 103; B p 224; C i 225.   10 B xv 116; C x 214.   11 A x 8; B ix 8; C xi 134.   12 B xiii 449; C viii 109.   13 B xiv 276, cf. C xvii 118. 14 B xv 55; C xvii 217; cf. B xiv 122; C xvi 303.   15 B xv 373; C xviii 113.

were supposed to be acquainted with philosophy and "physic,"
a term which was mainly used in the later Middle Ages in the
sense of *medicine*[1]. Natural science received little attention[2];
but in addition to lawful branches of knowledge[3], numerous
black arts were practised. Such churchmen as Langland did
not approve of the experiments made in alchemy by Albertus
Magnus[4]; they discouraged the study of alchemy, geomancy,
sorcery, necromancy and "perimancie," or pyromancy.

In this age when the entire population lived in fear of a return
of the Black Death, it might be supposed that learned men
would try to combat the enemy who

> cam dryvende after · and al to doust passhed
> Kynges and kny3tes · kayseres and popes;
> Lered ne lewed · he let no man stonde,
> That he hitte evene · that evere stired after.
> Many a lovely lady · and lemmanes of knyghtes
> Swouned and swelted · for sorwe of Dethes dyntes[5].

But in spite of the visitations of the plague, the measures
taken by town officials to safeguard public health met with
little support from contemporary scientists. No marked advance
in the study of natural science was made until many years after
Langland's death. According to his account the early theories
had undergone little change. Galen's account of the human
body was still accepted; and Langland refers to the four elements of the body; earth, air, wind and water[6]. The horror of
the pestilence strengthened that popular belief in a connection
between the human body and the forces of the universe, which
caused diseases to be attributed to planetary influence and to
supernatural agency[7]. Priests and moralists seem to have encouraged this belief; and though Langland dates many abuses
"sithen the pestilence[8]," he records that

> thuse pestilences
> Was for pure synne · to punyshe the puple[9].

Men were inclined to place great confidence in miraculous

---

1 See the quotations given by Hilarin Felder in his *Studien im Franziskanerorden* (Freiburg i/B, 1904, pp. 391 ff.).   2 B xiii 14; C xvi 17.
3 B xii 225, cf. C xv 160.   4 A xi 153, 157; B x 208.   5 B xx 99,
cf. C xxiii 100.   6 A x 3; B ix 3; C xi 129.   7 B xx 79, 96; C xxiii
80, 97; Writings of John of Burgoyne or John of Bordeaux. See Creighton,
I, pp. 208 ff.   8 A P 81, x 185, xi 59; B P 84, ix 164, x 72; C I 82,
xi 272, xii 55; Wright, *Political Poems*, vol. I, p. 279, "On the Pestilence."
9 C vi 115, cf. A v 13, B v 13.

means of relief from physical infirmities[1]. Relics of holy men
were supposed to be invested with powers of healing, and many
such won world-wide fame. The reputation of St Radegund[2] as
a healer of "gounds," or running sores, was so firmly established
that the name of the disease was remodelled to the form in
which it occurs in *Piers Plowman*, "radegoundes." But sometimes the affliction, whatever it might be, was regarded as the
work of fiends, and men sought help from sorcerers and witches.
Haukyn had turned to them in desperation:

> I cacche the crompe · the cardiacle some tyme,
> Or an ague in suche an angre · and some tyme a fevre,
> That taketh me al a twelf-moneth · tyl that I despyse
> Lechecrafte of owre lorde · and leve on a wicche,
> And segge, that no clerke ne can · ne Cryste, as I leve,
> To the souter of Southwerke · or of Shordyche dame Emme!
> And segge, that no goddes worde · gaf me nevere bote,
> But thorw a charme had I chaunce · and my chief hele[3]!

In his use of his predecessor's remedies the physician had to
work in ignorance[4]; the grain of commonsense suggesting the
old prescription was often lost even when the ceremony was
superstitiously preserved. This accounts for the assertion
that the application of a dead scorpion heals a scorpion's sting[5];
for, possibly, at some period the discovery that venom of one
kind counteracts the effect of another variety, had led to the
formulation of a working principle "Like cures like." Experience and commonsense found a cause for the sickness of pam-
pered servants, namely, over-eating and over-drinking[6]; and the
discoveries of experience were recorded[7] in such rough sum-
maries as Langland's metrical list of the diseases accompanying
the pestilence as it came forth "out of the planetes":

> fevres and fluxes,
> Coughes, and cardiacles · crampes, and tothaches,
> Rewmes, and radegoundes · and roynouse scalles,
> Byles, and bocches · and brennyng agues;
> Frenesyes, and foule yveles[8].

In spite of the limitations of their knowledge the leeches

---

1 B XIII 248; C XVI 218; Froissart, Globe Edition, Pt 2, chaps. XXVII,
p. 335; Walsingham, *Historia Anglicana*, II 183, 188, 189. 2 B XX 82;
C XXIII 83. 3 B XIII 335, cf. C VII 78. 4 A V 101; B V 123, cf.
C VII 88; B XX 173, 308; C XXIII 174, 310. 5 B XVIII 153; C XXI 158.
6 A VII 245; B VI 260; C IX 272. 7 A XII 84; B XVII 66; C XX 66.
8 B XX 80, cf. C XXIII 81.

prospered and enraged the moralists by demanding beforehand fees which they were unable to earn[1]. Disease was a source of income and Langland hints that the remedy for the trickery practised by these impostors lay in the hands of the sufferers:

> Let not sir Surfet · sitten at thi bord; says Hunger,
> ...ʒif thou diʒete the thus · I dar legge bothe myn eres,
> That Fisyk schal his forred hod · for his foode sulle,
> And eke his cloke of Calabre · with knappes of gold,
> And beo fayn, be my feith · his fisyk to lete,
> And leorne to labre with lond · leste lyflode faile;
> Ther beoth mo lyʒers then leches · ur lord hem amende!
> Thei don men dyʒen thoruʒ heor drinke · er destenye wolde[2].

REGULARS

It was usual in the Middle Ages for such men and women as were weary of the irreligion and materialism of contemporary society to withdraw to the cloister. Not that such people with real "vocations" formed the majority at any but exceptional times or exceptional places; but there was no time at which there was not a considerable sprinkling of truly religious people among the cloistered clergy. In freeing themselves from worldly responsibilities they generally found peace and opportunity for exercising pious sentiments and deeds. Their interests were, however, narrowed; and, as the monastic orders increased in numbers and power, the relations between laity and regular clergy[3] became strained.

Langland held that only strict obedience to "St Gregory's Rule" justified monastic seclusion[4]; and, for this reason, he regretted the acquisition of considerable estates by the regular clergy. The administration of their affairs compelled certain members of the order to leave the cloister. Upon re-entering the world vows and rules were too often forgotten, and the monk adopted the manners of a secular landowner. He rode his palfrey from town to town with "a bidowe or a baselard[5]" at his side; and his conversation was ill-suited to a holy man. He is described as

1 A II 199; B II 223, XX 175; C III 233, IV 302, XXIII 176; Creighton, *History of Epidemics in Britain*, I, p. 209.   2 A VII 252, cf. B VI 267; C IX 277.   3 The "regular" clergy, in medieval parlance, are the "Religious"; *i.e.* the cloistered clergy—Monks, Canons Regular, Friars and Nuns—as distinguished from the "secular" clergy, whose work and life lies in the "world," *i.e.* outside the cloister *in saeculo*.   4 A XI 201; B X 292; C VI 147; Gilles li Muisis, Langlois, *Moralistes*, p. 312.   5 A XI 211.

a ryder · a rowmer bi stretes,
A leder of lovedayes · and a londe-bugger,
A priker on a palfray · fro manere to manere,
An heep of houndes at his ers · as he a lorde were.
And but if his knave knele · that shal his cuppe brynge,
He loureth on hym and axeth hym · who tau3te hym curteisye[1]?

The monk's business, according to Langland, is to obey his own Rule, and not to wander abroad on pilgrimages to Rome or Rocamadour[2]. Hermits, monks and friars may attain to the holiness of the apostles[3]; whereas the "poor preacher," by following no known Rule and possessing no property, forfeits all respect[4]. In later life his fear, that the orders were ruled by ambition and avarice, seems to have been confirmed, and he omitted his unfriendly comment on the poor preacher[5]. He no longer asserts that pottage, penny-ale, bread and simple fare satisfied the man who had taken monastic vows[6]. He advises men to refrain from rendering the religious orders independent by these gifts of money and estates[7]. In some cases such property was treated as a mere source of income[8]; and the poet mentions that certain parish churches, appropriated to religious orders, were so neglected that rain fell on the altars[9].

Religious were therefore called upon to reduce their wealth and increase their spiritual influence by refusing the alms of unjust men and women[10]. Langland felt that, unless they reformed themselves, the laity would be called upon to punish them[11]. The fate of the Templars held a grave warning for any order which worshipped treasure rather than truth[12]; and in *Piers Plowman* there was a bold suggestion that the king and his barons might give the death-blow to monasticism:

there shal come a kyng · and confesse 3ow religiouses,
And bete 3ow, as the bible telleth · for brekynge of 3owre reule,
And amende monyales · monkes and chanouns,
And putten hem to her penaunce · *ad pristinum statum ire,*

1 B x 306, cf. C vi 157; Wright, "Complaint of the Ploughman," pp. 307, 334.   2 B iv 121, xii 36; C v 117.   3 B xv 409.   4 B vi 151 (see Skeat, *Note*), cf. B xi 278, C xiv 101.   5 B xv 506; C iv 203, xviii 206.
6 B xv 310.   7 B x 312, xv 315; C vi 164, xviii 54.   8 B x 313; C vi 165; Wyclif, iii, p. 380, "Fifty Heresies and Errors of the Friars," cap. xvii.
9 The reports of episcopal and archidiaconal visitations show that this was no mere figure of speech; see, for instance, the cases recorded in the "Visitation of the Archdeaconry of Totnes in 1342" (*Eng. Hist. Rev.* Jan. 1911, pp. 108 ff.).   10 B xv 302, 304; C xviii 35, 44.   11 A v 39; B v 48, x 266; C vi 146.   12 B xv 509; C xviii 209.

And barounes with erles beten hem · thorugh *beatus-virres* techynge,
That here barnes claymen · and blame ʒow foule:
Hij in curribus et hij in equis; ipsi obligati sunt, etc.,
And thanne freres in here freitoure · shal fynden a keye
Of Costantynes coffres · in which is the catel
That Gregories god-children · han yvel dispended.
And thanne shal the abbot of Abyndoun · and alle his issu for evere
Have a knokke of a kynge · and incurable the wounde.
. . . .
Ac ar that kynge come · Cayme shal awake.
Ac Dowel shal dyngen hym adoune · and destruyen his myʒte[1].

All orders were not equally guilty. Though the monks were sometimes worldly-minded[2] and neglected almsgiving, they did not threaten the well-being of the nation. Some were loyal to their Rule and set laymen a fine example of discipline. Order and regularity seem to have been usual in a well-governed monastery[3].

Monkes and monyals · and alle men of religioun
Her ordre and her reule wil · to han a certeyne noumbre[4].

The authorities, that is, exercised supervision over a limited number of monks. The chapter ruled with a firm hand and punished insubordinate monks by birching[5]. Living was simple; inferior fish and weak ale seem to have formed a great part of the diet. The Friday fast of bread and water was observed. Alms were sought only by specially appointed "obediencers[6]."

Nuns or "moniales" shared the power and wealth of the monks[7]; but Langland is less favourable to them than to his own sex. He mentions an abbess, closely connected with Wrath, who delighted in uncharitable gossip[8]; and nuns who quarrelled freely with each other[9]. Behaviour and language, intolerable in any decent household, were known within the convent and the morality was not above suspicion[10]. The laity supported[11] Pope Gregory IX (not *saint* Gregory as the author imagines) in his refusal to permit abbesses or prioresses to hear confession, lest they should on the first day become "infamis[12]."

Piers Plowman reflects the common contemporary feeling that monasticism needed reform. Both monks and canons regular

---

1 B x 317, cf. C vi 169.   2 A xi 208; B iii 132, x 306; C iv 169, vi 76, 157.   3 A v 233; B v 460; C viii 67.   4 B xx 262, cf. C xxiii 264.   5 B v 169 ff.; C vii 151 ff.   6 C vi 91.   7 B xx 262; C vi 76, xxiii 264.   8 B v 153; C vii 128.   9 C vii 137.   10 C vii 141. 11 B v 166.   12 *I.e.* fall under the ban of the Church for revealing the secrets of the confessional.

had deviated from the purity of their original rule[1]. But we gather a general impression that, in spite of their failings, monks, nuns and canons had, by preserving high ideals and encouraging interest in spiritual and intellectual matters, accomplished some real part of the work they had undertaken. The reference to the "unthende-fish," the "fieble ale" and the stern realities of corporal punishment could not otherwise be explained. It is obvious that Langland, like other of his contemporaries[2], regards the mendicant orders as the most corrupt of the regular clergy and a real menace to social life; though it is when speaking of them that he says:

> me is loth, thow ich Latyn knowe · to lacky eny secte,
> For alle we ben brethren · thauh we be diversliche clothede[3].

In the Field Full of Folk he describes how

> freris · alle the foure ordres,
> Preched the peple · for profit of hem-selven,
> Glosed the gospel · as hem good lyked,
> For coveitise of copis · construed it as thei wolde.
> Many of this maistres freris · mowe clothen hem at lykyng,
> For here money and marchandise · marchen togideres.
> For sith charite hath be chapman · and chief to shryve lordes,
> Many ferlis han fallen · in a few 3eris.
> But holychirche and hii · holde better togideres,
> The moste myschief on molde · is mountyng wel faste[4].

The order of the Paulines[5] was also corrupt; for

> Pieres the pardonere · of Paulynes doctrine[6],

was one of Wrong's most active supporters, and his comrades were the steeds who bore Civil Law to Westminster to defend Lady Mede[7]. To the benefactors who filled the friary church windows with glass[8] or supplied the friars with measures of wheat[9], Langland uttered the warning:

> Thauh thou be founden in fraternite · a-mong the foure ordres,
> And habbe indulgence i-doubled · bote Dowel the helpe,
> I nolde 3eve for thi pardoun · one pye-hele[10]!

1 A x 109; B xv 315; C xviii 54; Wyclif, iii, 345, 346, "The Church and Her Members," cap. iv.   2 *Piers Plowman's Crede*, Song against Friars.—Wright, i, 266.   3 C xvi 78.   4 B P 58, cf. A P 55, C i 56.   5 These "Paulines" seem to have been the same as the Crutched Friars, who were not numerous in England and whose history is obscure.   6 B ii 108, cf. A ii 76, C iii 110.   7 A ii 152; B ii 177.   8 A iii 49; B iii 48; C iv 51.   9 A iii 41; B iii 40; C iv 42.   10 A viii 179, cf. B vii 192, C x 343.

Though there were

> Maistres of the menours · men of grete wittes[1]

whose discussions Langland feared as tending to heresy[2], the friars were not above admitting to their orders undesirable persons for as long as pleased them. Liar remained for a time with the minstrels, but

> Freres with feir speches · fetten him thennes;
> For knowynge of comers · kepten him as a frere;
> Bote he hath leve to lepen out · as ofte as him lyketh,
> And is wel-come whon he wole · and woneth with hem ofte[3].

As Langland's admiration for the well-organised life of the monastery seems to increase, so his hostility to the friars seems to become more marked. There was no limit to their number and they had no regular system of government[4]. Friars swarmed in every country:

> thei ben men on this molde · that moste wyde walken,
> And knowen contrees, and courtes · and many kynnes places,
> Both prynces paleyses · and pore mennes cotes[5].

The friar was compared with the fiddler; both were ready

>   to seke festes,
> Homelich at other mennes houses · and hatyen her owne[6].

The mention of the friar in Beton's tavern[7] and the picture of the master-friar—the friar who had taken a Doctorate in Divinity—suggest that whenever possible the impostors threw off even the appearance of holiness. This master, attended by his servant, made his way through the crowd of pilgrims and beggars to the chief table on the daïs. Here he devoured the richest food and finest wines at a rate which amazed humble folk at the side tables:

> He eet many sondry metes · mortrewes and puddynges,
> Wombe-cloutes and wylde braune · egges yfryed with grece.
> Thanne seide I to my-self · so Pacience it herde,
> "It is nou3t foure dayes that this freke · bifor the den of Poules,
> Preched of penaunces · that Poule the apostle suffred,
> *In fame & frigore* · and flappes of scourges[8]."

---

1 A ɪx 9; B vɪɪɪ 9; C xɪ 9.   2 A xɪ 58; B x 71; C xɪɪ 54.   3 A ɪɪ 205,
cf. B ɪɪ 229, C ɪɪɪ 239.   4 B xx 265; C xxɪɪɪ 267.   5 B vɪɪɪ 14, cf.
C xɪ 14.   6 B x 92.   7 B vɪ 74; C ɪx 73.   8 B xɪɪɪ 62,
cf. C xvɪ 66.

When the dinner was finished he

> rody as a rose · rubbed his chekes,
> Coughed and carped

and told his companions that Dowel was to

> Do non yvel to thine evenecrystene · nou3t by thi powere.

It was useless to ask for example as well as precept; he paid no attention to the writer's remark:

> "By this day, sire doctour," quod I · "thanne be 3e nou3t in Dowel;
> For 3e han harmed us two · in that 3e eten the puddyng,
> Mortrewes, and other mete · and we no morsel hade!
> And if 3e fare so in 3owre fermorie · ferly me thinketh,
> But chest be there charite shulde be · and 3onge childern dorste
> pleyne[1]!"

The hint as to the treatment of the sick friars was allowed to pass unanswered[2]. From the time that the friars indulged in the once forbidden pleasures of comfortable housing, fine clothing and superior education, their value as guardians of the poor decreased[3]. They needed money and accepted alms from any sinner[4]; they would have followed Antichrist himself, says the poet, for copes[5].

Langland attributes the zeal which led the great majority of friars to qualify for the priesthood to their greed for wealth[6]. Their services attracted idlers, as being the least exacting form of worship[7]; and their easy penances made them most popular confessors[8]. The friars, including the limitours, who begged for alms, and the lectors, or occasional preachers, seem to have taken advantage of the unsuspicious nature of their victims. Wrath confesses:

> On limitoures and listres · lesynges I ympid,
> Tyl thei bere leves of low speche · lordes to plese,
> And sithen thei blosmed obrode · in boure to here shriftes[9].

Sometimes the host who had admitted the confessor to the lady's bower found himself betrayed in his absence[10]. Possibly the very vices of which Langland complained encouraged perjured executors and officers of law-courts to

> fleen to the freres · as fals folke to Westmynstre[11].

---

1 B xiii 105, cf. C xvi 115.   2 Wyclif, iii, "Fifty Heresies and Errors of the Friars," cap. xxii.   3 B xv 75, 321; C xvii 235.   4 B xv 306. 5 B xx 57; C xxiii 58.   6 B xx 232; C xxiii 233.   7 B v 418; C viii. 27.   8 B xx 311; C xxiii 313.   9 B v 138.   10 B xx 341; C xxiii 343. 11 B xx 282, 288; C xxiii 284, 290.

When they were shriven they gave the friars

> A parcel to preye for hem · and maken hem murye
> With the remenant of the good · that other men byswonke,
> And suffre the dede in dette · to the day of dome[1].

Privileges were however reserved for wealthy sinners who could afford to pay large sums for letters of fraternity, as the documents admitting to privileges of the orders were called[2];

> while Fortune is thy frend · freres wollen the lovye,
> And fastne the in here fraternite · and for the by-seche
> To here priour provincial · hus pardon to have,
> And praye for the, pol by pol · yf thow be pecunyous[3].

Such friends of the orders presented roof and cloisters to the friary church, adorned the walls and had their names inscribed in the windows[4]; but Langland thought it necessary to remind the friars to sing due masses for the peace of their benefactors' souls[5].

Though the friars were said to hold the doctrine that

> alle thinges under hevene · ouȝte to ben in comune[6]

they lost no opportunity of enriching themselves. Langland observed

> how that freris folwed · folke that was riche,
> And folke that was pore · at litel prys thei sette,
> And no corps in her kirkeȝerde · ne in her kyrke was buryed,
> But quikke he biquethe hem auȝte · or shulde helpe quyte her dettes[7].

They preferred burying dead Christians to enrolling new members of the Church on account of the lavish almsgiving at the funeral ceremonies[8]. If a wealthy man were sick, the friar hastened to his bedside and overwhelmed him with attentions.

Parish priests protested loudly against these practices, which robbed them of part of their income[9]. They denounced the friars in the hearing of their congregation and the friars retorted only too readily. By their study of logic, law, natural science[10] and

---

1 C xxiii 291, cf. B xx 289.   2 Wyclif, i 60, Sermons; iii 377, 378, "Fifty Heresies and Errors of the Friars," cap. xv; iii 420, "De Blasphemia, contra fratres."   3 C xiii 8, cf. B xi 54.   4 B iii 60; C iv 64, cf. B v 269, xiv 198; C vii 288, xvii 41.   5 B xiii 45; C xvi 51.   6 B xx 274; C xxiii 276.   7 B xiii 7, cf. C xvi 9.   8 B xi 73, 76, xx 322; C xiii 22, xxiii 324; Wyclif, iii 374, "Fifty Heresies and Errors of the Friars," cap. x; Wright, *Political Poems*, "On the Council of London," i 257.   9 B v 143, cf. C vii 120.   10 No direct mention, but friar-confessor compared to a leech.

theology[1] many of them had won the titles of master and doctor, and were more than a match for the parish priest[2]. Laymen who were weary of the well-worn themes of discourse at the parish church[3] flocked to hear the more learned or pretentious sermons of the friars at St Paul's and elsewhere[4]. The enemies of the mendicants accused them in vain of fostering unbelief amongst ignorant and learned men alike, by bold remarks on the Trinity[5]. The only weak point in the friar's eloquence which the crowd noticed was that these preachers of self-denial had fat cheeks and fine appetites[6]. The poet says, however, that their "Apocalipsis Goliæ" and St Averay excused this inconsistency.

Langland's remedy against the power of these corrupt orders consisted in depriving the friars of their chief claim to sanctity. Their vow of poverty had originally won for them the support of rich and poor[7]; and now, though they remained the "poor brothers[8]" only in name, they still met with sympathy and pity. Langland suggests that they should cease to profess what they no longer practised, and that they should live, like other Religious, upon regular endowments; he believed that if the monks' wealth were distributed, the friars would thus be enabled to live without begging[9].

The few additions to the last version show that the poet still marked the rapid deterioration of the mendicant orders. He mentions the fifth order of friars, which Skeat is probably right in identifying as the Crutched Friars[10]; but it is doubtful whether this allusion contains, as he suspects, an indication of the date of the third version. Prelates[11] began to fear that this usurpation of the parish priests' duties was the first step towards a mendicant supremacy in the Church. Orthodox commentaries on the Gospel were rejected by the friars[12], and the Church's supporters were advised by the poet to treat them almost as enemies[13]. Meanwhile the idlers and vagabonds, envying the success of fat-cheeked deceivers in fine clothing, sought admission to the orders[14].

The earliest English minorites had attempted to adhere rigidly

---

1 B XIII 172, XX 271; C XVI 85, 171, XXIII 273. 2 A P 59; B P 62; C I 60. 3 B XV 71; C XVII 233. 4 B X 71, XII 19, XIII 65; C XII 54, XVI 69. 5 B X 74, XV 70; C XII 57, XVII 232. 6 B XIII 65, 90; C X 208, XVI 69, 99. 7 B X 381; C XXIII 383. 8 B XV 321. 9 B X 323; C VI 174. 10 C IX 191, X 343, XVI 81. 11 C VII 120. 12 C I 59. 13 C I 64. 14 C IX 73, X 208.

to the rule as it had existed in Southern Europe, but had been obliged to make certain variations. From the first, churchmen recognised the impossibility of leading in a cold climate the life of an Eastern anchorite. Labourers willingly undertook to provide food for the ascetic who spent his life in prayer and penance, partaking of one meal daily and never leaving his cell except to go on pilgrimage[1]. Even then the hermit suffered great privations and was regarded by the community as a self-denying and holy man. In the fourteenth century genuine hermits seem to have been as rare as holy friars:

> Grete lobies and longe · that loth were to swynke,
> Clothede hem in copis · to be knowe fro othere,
> And made hem-selve eremytes · hure eise to have[2].

The number of recluses was unlimited, and the pretenders assumed the hermit's cope and staff and travelled with their evil companions from shrine to shrine[3], escaping from work except in times of great extremity[4]. The hermit's garb became a familiar object in every crowd and was regarded with suspicion[5].

At the time he first revised his poem, when the poet seems to have developed a strong feeling for law and order[6], he taxed the anchorites with having no rule and owing obedience to no man. He also disapproved of their begging to supplement the contents of the alms-box outside their cell[7]. He sighed in vain for the Eastern saints who had been sustained by heavenly means[8].

Formerly the anchorite's chief object had been to escape from temptation[9] by renouncing

> londe and lordshep · and lykynges of the body[10].

In Langland's day this sacrifice was seldom made[11]; for the hermits were usually ignorant men of low birth who, inspired with the spirit of emulation by the sight of the fat cheeks of "faitours in frere clothynge," decided to exchange a laborious trade for a more profitable occupation[12]:

> these eremytes that edefyen thus · by the hye weyes,
> Whilom were workmen · webbes and taillours,

1 A P 28, VII 134; B P 28, VI 147; C I 30, IX 146.   2 A P 52; B P 55; C I 53.   3 A P 50; B P 53; C I 51.   4 A VII 177; B VI 190; C IX 183. 5 A P 3; B P 3; C I 3.   6 B XIII 285.   7 B XIII 30, XV 208.   8 B XV 269; C XVIII 6.   9 C X 196.   10 C X 202.   11 C VI 4.   12 C X 140; Jusserand, *English Wayfaring Life in the Middle Ages*, p. 147, quotes Rutebeuf, *Le Dit de frère Denise*.

And carters knaves · and clerkus with-oute grace,
Helden ful hungry hous · and hadde much defaute,
Long labour and lyte wynnynge · and atte laste aspiden,
That faitours in frere clothynge · hadde fatte chekus[1].

From the hermitage—usually a well-built cell by the high-road or in the lower quarters of the town, "in borwes a-mong brewesters[2]"—the anchorites set out to beg in churches and public places. Langland seems to have met them in the neighbourhood of his cot on Cornhill and learnt to mistrust them[3]. Their earnings were sometimes spent among drunken revellers in the tavern.

The last class of dependents of the Church of Rome were the beadsmen, who profited by the substitution of money payments for virtuous thoughts and deeds. The beadsman[4], though usually a pauper, escaped inclusion among beggars by offering prayers in return for alms[5]. In appearance he resembled a beggar[6] and though he was originally supposed to possess special powers of intercession, Langland doubted the efficacy of prayers of beadsmen of his day[7].

1 C x 203.   2 C x 188, 189.   3 C vi 4, vii 368.   4 Cf. A iii
47; B iii 41, 46; C iv 43, 48.   5 C iv 276.   6 B xv 199.
7 B xv 420.

II

SECULAR GOVERNMENT

KINGS, LORDS AND COMMONS

O F the two kings known personally to Langland, Edward III
represented most satisfactorily the typical monarch. The
cat and kitten of the fable inevitably suggest Edward III and
his grandson Richard II. The commons feared him, since he

cam whan hym lyked,
And overlepe hem ly3tlich · and lau3te hem at his wille,
And pleyde with hem perilouslych · and possed hem aboute[1].

But they respected his firm rule; for as the sober citizen, in the
form of "a mous that moche good couthe," declares

There the catte is a kitoun · the courte is ful elyng[2].

Similarly the king who tries Lady Mede resembles Edward III[3].
But when Richard II came to the throne, though, in his good or
bad moods, he does not seem to have impressed the poet by his
regal bearing, some of the old details were omitted[4]—possibly as
being out-of-date—and a few new references were added. The
new references allude chiefly to financial trouble. Reason suggests that, should the king redress the grievances of his subjects,
he should be rewarded:

ich dar legge my lyf · that Love wol lene the sulver,
To wage thyne, and help wynne · that thow wilnest after,
More than al thy marchauns · other thy mytrede bisshopes,
Other Lumbardes of Lukes · that lyven by lone as Jewes[5].

He is also cautioned against selling territory acquired in battle
by the commons and warned that the commons will continue to
displease him while he bears poor men's "bras" to Calais[6].

In discussing the attributes of a king Langland inclines to a
democratic point of view[7]. Loyalty was not accompanied by
the superstitious veneration afterwards claimed by the Stuarts;

1 B P 149, cf. C I 168.   2 B P 190, cf. C I 204.   3 A III 99; B III 100;
C IV 127.   4 B XIII 175.   5 C V 191.   6 C IV 244, cf. A III 189;
B III 195.   7 Wright, *Political Songs*, p. 118, "Reign of Henry III,"
l. 907, note to p. 117; *Political Poems*, I, p. 278, "On the Times 1388."

the king was in effect the chief of the knights entrusted with the protection of the realm[1]. Though the relations between the personifications Do-wel, Do-bet and Do-best are not always distinct, we understand quite clearly what was expected of their monarch who might kill "with-oute synne[2]":

> Dowel and Dobet · and Dobest the thridde
> Crounede on to be kyng · and kepen ous alle,
> And reulen alle reaumes · by here thre wittes;
> Bote other-wise ne elles nat · bote as thei three assented[3].

The king was supposed to choose wise councillors and to see that the laws they framed were executed[4]; otherwise even the labourer did not hesitate to curse

> the kynge · and al his conseille after,
> Suche lawes to loke · laboreres to greve[5].

Wiser men murmured and it so were

> That I were kynge with crowne · to kepen a rewme,
> Shulde nevere wronge in this worlde · that I wite my3te,
> Ben unpunisshed in my powere · for peril of my soule!
> Ne gete my grace for giftes · so me God save!
> Ne for no mede have mercy · but mekenesse it make[6].

As a member of the Church the king was expected to attend the usual services[7]; for Scripture says

> Kynghod ne kny3thod · by nau3t I can awayte,
> Helpeth nou3t to heveneward · one heres ende[8].

But in the fourteenth century there was a difference of opinion as to how his duties of defender of Holy Church and the clergy were best performed[9]. From Langland's account it appears that enemies within the fold were a more serious menace than pagans, and he suggests that the king might possibly help directly to reform the ecclesiastical organisation[10].

The king was supposed to adapt his private life to suit the requirements of his subjects. He was endowed with a certain income to meet his expenses, since

> Hyt by-cometh for a kyng · that shal kepe a reame,
> To 3eve men mede · that meklyche hym serveth,
> To alienes, to alle men · to honoury hem with 3yftes[11].

1 A I 92; B I 94; C I 90.   **2** C xi 100, cf. A ix 91, B viii 99.   **3** C xi 102, cf. A ix 97, B viii 103.   **4** A iv 9, 152; B iv 9, 189; C v 9. **5** B vi 318, cf. A vii 302, C ix 340.   **6** B iv 137, cf. A iv 120, C v 134. **7** A v 1; B v 1; C vi 113.   **8** B x 333, cf. A xi 222.   **9** A viii 9; B vii 9; C x 9.   **10** A v 38; B v 47, x 317; C vi 145, 169.   **11** C iv 266, cf. A iii 202, B iii 208.

To this he was entitled by the services he performed for the nation:

> Ich am a kyng with corone · the comune to reule,
> And holychurch and clergie · fro corsede men to defenden.
> And yf me lacketh to lyve by · the lawe wol that ich take
> There ich may have hit hastelokest · for ich am hefd of lawe[1].

Payments due through "escheats[2]" and "waifs and strays[3]" (or money realised by such casual windfalls as, for instance, the sales of strayed cattle and property of deceased aliens) are mentioned as part of the royal income. The privilege of purveyance, originally intended for use in extraordinary circumstances, was continually abused[4]; false purveyors harassed impoverished subjects when the king's authority was not upheld[5]. Great inconvenience might be caused to the country by an extravagant monarch[6]; and royal officers exacted "year gifts" for themselves from men who dared not defy them[7].

When Langland revised his poem, he, like other contemporary writers[8], emphasised the dependence of the king on the will of the commons. He owed the strength of his position to the support of the knightly class and the commons:

> Thanne come there a kyng · kny3thod hym ladde,
> Mi3t of the comunes · made hym to regne[9].

Without the consent of these classes it was difficult for the king to act:

> Quod Conscience to the kynge · "but the comune wil assent,
> It is ful hard, bi myn hed · here-to to brynge it,
> Alle 3owre lige leodes · to lede thus evene[10]."

His authority was granted subject to common law[11]; and if he sinned he was liable to the usual penalty:

> *Spiritus iusticie* · spareth nat to spille
> Hem that beoth gulty · and for to corecte
> The kyng, and the kyng falle · in eny thynge gulty.
> For counteth he no kynges wraththe · when he in court sytteth
> To deme as a domesman; · adrad was he nevere,
> Nother of duk ne of deth · that he ne doth the lawe,
> For present other for preyoure · othere eny princes letteres;
> He dude equyte to alle · evene-forth hus knowynge[12].

1 C xxii 468, cf. B xix 463.   2 B iv 175; C v 169.   3 B P 94; C i 92.   4 B xix 255; C xxii 260.   5 A iv 35; B iv 48; C v 46. 6 A iii 148; B iii 152; C iv 191.   7 A iii 90; B iii 99; C iv 126, cf. B viii 52, xiii 184.   8 Wright, *Political Songs*, pp. 95, 115, 116. 9 B P 112, cf. C i 139.   10 B iv 182, cf. C v 176; see also B P 132; C i 152 ff.   11 B xix 474; C xxii 479.   12 C xxii 303, cf. B xix 298.

Thus he was subject to divine decree and the common law; but the poet, seeking complete harmony in the state[1], hoped his actions would be inspired by love not fear, since "the comune ys the kynges tresour[2]."

The king was supposed to enforce the code of laws drawn up by himself, the lords and the commons, when they had first adjusted the duties of each section of society and decided the rights governing possession of property[3]. Definite limits confined the king's power in the law courts[4]; but custom permitted him to pardon a condemned felon at the foot of the gallows by which he happened to pass[5]. In time of war, the king, as the leader of the people, chose and commanded knights and officers of the army[6]:

> the kynde is of a kny3t · other for a kynge to be take,
> And among here enemys · in morteils bateles
> To be culled and overcome · the comune to defende[7].

Though he could make freemen or thralls of his captives[8] and might bestow lordship on whomsoever he chose[9], he was at all times expected to observe the principles of chivalry.

The fable of the cat and mice is quoted to prove that the sufferings caused by an individual ruler's caprices were only less terrible than rebellion. Religious scruples did not prevent Christian kings from waging bitter wars[10], and clerks could be found to justify the king's actions by misconstruing phrases[11]. At such times the commons

> comen to a conseille · for here comune profit;

and discussed the situation. As long as sufficient occupation could be found for the monarch all was well; for, as the mouse declared,

> The while he caccheth conynges · he coveiteth nou3t owre caroyne,
> But fet hym al with venesoun · defame we hym nevere[12].

But, even when they suffered most, the commons agreed that a ruler was indispensable; like the rats and mice they could not agree:

> For many mannus malt · we mys wolde destruye,
> And also 3e route of ratones · rende mennes clothes,
> Nere that cat of that courte · that can 3ow overlepe;
> For had 3e rattes 3owre wille · 3e couthe nou3t reule 3owre-selve[13].

1 B IV 123; C V 119.   2 C VI 182, cf. B V 50.   3 B P 116, cf. C I 144 ff; B XIX 42; C XXII 42.   4 B XVII 303; C XX 285. 5 B XVIII 379; C XXI 426.   6 B XIX 29, XX 256; C XXII 29, XXIII 257. 7 C XVIII 289.   8 B XIX 32; C XXII 32.   9 C IV 317.   10 B XIII 175. 11 B IV 149.   12 B P 193.   13 B P 197, cf. C I 212.

Elsewhere Langland insists on the necessity of an impartial judge:

> comune cleymeth of a kyng · thre kynne thynges,
> Lawe, love, and leaute · and hym lord antecedent,
> Bothe here hefd and here kyng · haldyng with no partie,
> Bote stande as a stake · that styketh in a muyre
> By-twyne two londes · for a trewe marke[1].

A curb was placed upon the monarch's actions by the necessity of accounting for them to the lords and commons in Parliament. The first version of *Piers Plowman* was written before the Good Parliament had begun its task; and the poet has little to say of its predecessor's work. He merely remarks on the presence of barons in the "Field Full of Folk," and laments the greed and consequent lack of faith among temporal lords[2]. He mentions that earls served amongst the lords as councillors, but does not refer to their duties[3]. Nothing is said of the commons.

In the second version the lord is reminded that he should defend the laws of the realm[4]. Barons and earls, as members of the king's council, were expected to protect public interests even when this entailed the correction of the clergy and redistribution of ecclesiastical property[5]—one of several points on which Langland, though no Lollard, agrees heartily with Wyclif. The supposed champions of popular interests seem to have despised poor men's advice, and tried to banish justice from the king's council by framing unjust laws[6].

There was one strong link between lords and commons, which is mentioned in the final version. It was possible for "loreles to be lordes and lewede men techeres[7]"; and Langland regrets that

> bondemenne barnes · han be mad bisshopes,
> And barnes bastardes · han ben archidekenes,
> And sopers and here sones · for selver han be knyghtes,
> And lordene sones here laborers · and leid here rentes to wedde,
> For the ryght of this reame · ryden a-ȝens oure enemys,
> In confort of the comune · and the kynges worshep,
> And monkes and moniales · that mendinauns sholden fynde,
> Han mad here kyn knyghtes · and knyghtfees purchased,
> Popes and patrones · poure gentil blod refuseth,
> And taken Symondes sone · seyntewarie to kepe[8].

1 C iv 381.   2 A p 96, ii 17, iii 150; B p 216, ii 22, iii 162; C i 219, iii 21.   3 A iv 152; B iv 189.   4 B ii 22; C iii 21.   5 B x 321, xv 526; C vi 173, xviii 227; Wyclif, iii 213, "Church Temporalities"; iii 478, Tract xxix; "On the Twenty-five Articles," point xiv.   6 B iii 296, xiv 307, xx 128; C xvii 145, xxiii 129.   7 C xv 20.   8 C vi 70.

The regulations of guild and town proved the commons' care for their own interests[1]; and officers were specially appointed to protect them from tyrannical government. The rapid development of the law courts was probably the outcome of the aggressive attitude which the citizens assumed if one of their number sustained injury to his person[2] or his property:

Shal nother kyng ne kny3t · constable ne meyre
Over-cark the comune · ne to the court sompne,
Ne putte men in panell · ne do men plighte here treuthe;
Bote after the dede that ys ydo · the dome shal recorde[3].

The citizens, superior to the labouring classes, concentrated their energies on the organisation of labour and security of property[4]. The clergy accused them of caring only for material prosperity[5]. Honest members of society, when they tried to compete with their less scrupulous fellows, suffered by reason of the dishonest tricks in practice[6].

Langland was very anxious that, during Richard's reign, the "social contract[7]" between king and commons should not be violated[8]. He warned his fellow-countrymen of the danger of quarrelling amongst themselves or failing to fulfil their promises of loyalty:

Let no kynne consail · ne covetyse 3ow departe,
That on wit and on wil · alle 3oure wardes kepe[9].

MAGISTRATES AND COURTS OF LAW

The law of the land was only second in importance to the Edicts of the Church. Only in time of extreme necessity might the law be disregarded. Then as the poet declares "Nede ne hath no lawe[10]"; each man having a natural right to such food and raiment as would keep body and soul together. There is a curious and obscure allusion to "Folvyles lawes[11]," which may possibly refer, as Skeat interprets it, to the frequency of a sort of Lynch law.

Westminster was the usual home of English law, sometimes alluded to as "Westminster law[12]." Langland records[13] that,

---

1 B p 115.   2 B iv 80; C v 76.   3 C iv 471, cf. B iii 313.
4 B p 118, 122; C i 144.   5 B xix 448; C xxii 453.   6 B iii 163;
C iv 202, 207.   7 C i 147.   8 C iv 381.   9 C vi 185.
10 B xx 10; C xxiii 10.   11 B xix 241; C xxii 247.   12 C xi 239.
13 A ii 113; B ii 143; C iii 157.

through the corruption of officials, all the wisdom of Westminster was frequently perverted to serve wealth rather than justice[1]. The proceedings of the king in council are described in the enquiry, held at Westminster[2], into Lady Mede's behaviour. Though some details are obscured by the allegory, and great prominence is given to the greed of officials, the chief characteristics of the trial are preserved.

The trial began as an enquiry into the suitability of a match which would place great wealth at the disposal of enemies of the state, and ended with an examination of the use previously made of the property concerned. Before the trial, the prisoner was besieged in her private chamber by justices and clerks who offered their influence and advice for money[3]. The king first attempted to settle matters by arbitration, and requested the lady to marry a knight in whom he had perfect confidence[4]. She agreed; but the knight refused her hand and altered the course of the enquiry by the charges he brought against her. Her petition to defend herself was granted; and for a time her skilful pleading won the king's sympathy. A new councillor was summoned to the court, and received with great honour by the king[5]. Another case was brought forward[6]; and the Lady Mede, by interfering illegally to save one of her friends, proved that the charges brought against her were well-founded. Though she attempted to win the sympathy of the officials, the court, led by the new councillor, decided against her[7]; and she was obliged to withdraw with her few remaining friends[8]. The king in his gratitude appointed his new adviser to be Chancellor of the Exchequer and ruler in his parliament. The knight who had revealed Mede's guilt was made a King's Justice.

Nothing of the proceedings in other courts is mentioned in *Piers Plowman*. The poet refers[9] in general terms to the absence of charity among commoners in court and states that the king could not save a guilty man in response to appeals[10]; though documents bearing the privy seal received special attention[11]. Langland feels that real justice requires that both the king's

---

1 A III 12; B III 12, XX 131, 282; C IV 13, XXIII 132, 284.   2 A III; B III; C IV.   3 A III 13, 27; B III 13, 26; C IV 14, 27.   4 A III 95; B III 103; C IV 127.   5 A IV 7; B IV 7; C V 7.   6 A IV 81; B IV 94; C V 90.   7 B IV 152; C V 148.   8 B IV 167; C V 162.   9 C XVII 359.   10 B XVII 303; C XX 285.-   11 A III 141; B III 145; C IV 183.

council and the common folks' opinion should receive attention[1].

When the king passed sentence upon Wrong he

> comaundede a constable · to casten him in irens;
> "He ne schal this seven ʒer · seon his feet ones[2]."

Similarly, he threatened Mede with imprisonment "In the castel of Corf[3]." Other punishments mentioned are mercements or fines[4], outlawry[5] and hanging[6]. No felon might be hanged a second time, if the hangman failed to carry out the sentence[7]. If a householder perished on the gallows, though he were a franklin[8], his son lost the inheritance. Pillory, "pynyngestole[9]" and stocks[10] were punishments meted out to untrustworthy citizens by persons in authority such as mayors and mace-bearers.

Possibly the fact that magistrates were usually chosen from the wealthier and better educated classes was regarded as a rough guarantee of their honesty[11]. The precaution seems to have been insufficient; for bribes sometimes altered the course of the law[12], and a whispered promise of money changed the sentence as it passed from the justice's lips[13].

Laymen could not perceive if a charter were written in false Latin, "peynted par-entrelignarie," or interlined, or in danger of being challenged by reason of omissions[14]; and they were inclined to overrate the importance of men who had mastered the intricacies of charters and letters-patent[15], by which position and wealth might be claimed. The sergeant-at-law[16] received his title from the king and was distinguished "atte barre" by his silken hood[17]. He also wore a costly "ray-robe," i.e. striped garment, and fur on his cloak and "*paveylon*," or hood[18]. He expected large fees for his services; and the commons remarked unfavourably on any of their number who neglected to salute him in the street[19]; probably because they feared "pillories and pynynge-

<hr>

1 B xx 29; C xxiii 29. 2 A iv 72, cf. B iv 85, C v 81. 3 C iv 140.
4 C ii 159, v 182. 5 B xvii 102. 6 C xi 240. 7 B xviii 377;
C xxi 424. 8 C xi 240. 9 B iii 78. 10 B iv 108, v 585; C v 103,
viii 223. 11 A viii 172; B vii 185, xiv 287; C x 336, xvii 125.
12 A iii 13, 151; B iii 13, 154; C iv 14, 193. 13 B xx 133; C xxiii
134. 14 B xi 296; C xiv 117. 15 A ii 58; B ii 68, xvii 10; C iii
69, xx 12. 16 A p 84; B p 210; C i 159. 17 A iii 276; B iii 293;
C iv 451. 18 A iii 277; B iii 294, cf. C iv 452. 19 B xv 8.

stoles[1]." Notaries[2], inspired by their superiors' success, practised all kinds of deceptions upon men who sought their help[3]. When they appeared at Westminster, their pockets were lined with bribes[4]. Other officials, unskilled in legal matters, carried out by force the sentence pronounced by the judge. Sergeants-at-arms conducted the prisoner to the court[5]. The fortress in which the prisoners were confined was entrusted to the care of the constable, who was usually a knight[6]. Langland suggested[7] that the constable was over-zealous in enforcing the king's com-mandments by pillory and fetters. The hangman of Tyburn is briefly referred to in the description of Beton's tavern[8].

In secular as in ecclesiastical courts the officials who served writs had acquired an unenviable reputation. "Sisours" rivalled summoners in their greed[9]. Like a certain class of men who regularly attended inquests[10], they were frequently forsworn; and some of their number, according to Langland's account of "Thomme Two-tonge," "nevre swore treuthe[11]." They paid the friars to pray for their souls, whilst they made merry with other men's property[12]. In the country, sheriffs and their officers per-formed the duties of punishing unscrupulous tradesmen by pillory and "pynynge-stole[13]"; and, wherever they travelled, on horseback or in a comfortable "saumbury," or litter, the system of bribery continued[14]. Langland accuses them of regarding illegal profits as a regular source of income[15].

The commons were taught to speak with reverence of guardians of the law[16]; and 'prentices of law are mentioned together with priests and preachers[17]. Langland, however, advises wise clerks[18] and "wytty men of lawe[19]" to abandon their evil practices.

---

1 C IV 78.   **2** A II 82.   **3** A II 97; B II 126, XX 270; C III 139, XXIII 272.   **4** A II 115, 144; B II 145, 166; C III 159.   **5** A III 96, 210; B III 101, 216, XIX 335; C IV 274, XXII 341.   **6** A X 16; B IX 17, XX 213; C XI 142, XXIII 214. In a township the constable was—what he remained almost until the memory of living man—the semi-professional guardian of the law satirized by Shakespeare in Dogberry.   **7** B III 313; C IV 256, 471; A II 173, IV 72; B II 198, IV 85; C III 210, V 81.   **8** C VII 368.   **9** A II 46, 135, 142, III 129; B II 58, 62, 164, III 133; C III 59, 63, 179, IV 171.   **10** B XIX 367; C XXII 372.   **11** B XX 161; C XXIII 162.   **12** B XX 288; C XXIII 290.   **13** B IV 168; C IV 78, V 164; "A Lytell Geste of Robyn Hode," Fyfth and Syxte Fyttes, *The Ballad Book*, ed. Allingham.   **14** A II 130; B II 58, 163; C III 59, 178.   **15** A III 130; B III 134; C IV 172.   **16** C IX 85.   **17** B XIX 226; C XXII 231.   **18** A III 91.   **19** C XXI 357.

He asserts that they undertook the defence of the most corrupt
sinner for money[1]:

> Wisdam and wit nou · is not worth a russche
> But hit beo cardet with covetise · as clothers doth heor wolle,
> That conterfeteth disseites · and conspiret wronges,
> And ledeth forth a loveday · to lette the trewthe;
> That suche craftes cunnen · to counseil beoth i-clept,
> And ben served as syres · that serveth the devel[2].

It was difficult to incite the clergy against men of law; for the
legal profession was closely connected with the Church[3], ecclesiastics holding high offices in the law courts. The methods of civil
law[4] were tolerated by the Pope[5]; and, in spite of rivalry, the
clergy and representatives of secular law combined to hide each
other's crimes[6]. Those who came into contact with them imitated their methods; and the poet[7] rejoiced to think that the
ill-gotten gains stood a good chance of being stolen and squan-
dered by executors. For to the frequent knavery of executors
Langland bears testimony as emphatically as his contemporaries[8].

Injustice might be wrought without actually breaking the
law; and even the king complained that, through corruption,
he lost many "escheats[9]." The principle "might is right" frequently held good through the working of "maintenance[10]." A
concrete instance of this is given in *Piers Plowman*. A powerful
lord[11] oppressed his neighbours, maintaining men to steal the
goods and murder any of the farmer's men who resisted them.
The victim could neither avenge himself nor defend his property,
since his own men were hopelessly inferior to his enemy's re-
tainers. The only hope of redress lay in appealing to king and
parliament. A just king might listen to the appeal; but a weak
or avaricious monarch, hoping to share the plunder, would
decide in favour of the stronger party. Enemies of public wel-

---

1 B IV 152; C V 67, 148; Cesarii *Dialogus Mirac.*, vol. II, p. 304.
2 A XI 17, cf. B X 17, C XII 14; Wright, *Political Songs*, "Poem on the
Times of Edward II."   3 B P 93; C I 91.   4 C III 243.   5 B XX
136; C XXIII 137. It must be remembered also that the Pope's own code,
Canon Law, was to a great extent based on the civil law of the Lower
Empire, as codified by Justinian.   6 A II 147; B II 169; C III 183,
XVIII 46.   7 B V 266; C VII 254.   8 B XII 258, XV 128, 243, XX
288; C XVII 277, XXIII 290.   9 B IV 175; C V 169.   10 A IV 42; B IV
55; C V 58; *Richard the Redeless*, Passus III 268.   11 Or possibly, as
Skeat suggests, a royal servant, taking advantage of the right of "pur-
veyance."

fare found protection in this system of maintenance; and usurers lent money to lords who promised them their support[1]. Seldom indeed is the word used in a good sense, as when the knight promises to "maintain[2]" the ploughman who provides him with food. "Maintenance" became practically synonymous with illegal protection. The mayor "maintained" retailers of food-stuffs who bribed him to suffer their deceptions[3]. Lady Mede is said to "maintain" priests and parsons against the law, by offer-ing bribes for their support[4]. In real life popes and prelates imitated her methods by offering presents to men that they might "maintain" their laws[5].

Through the custom of finding bail or "mainprise[6]," many guilty men escaped punishment and were released from prison upon the pretext that they made amends[7]. The person who pro-vided bail was called the "meynpernour[8]"; owing to the dangers attending this practice, a prisoner of particularly bad character was not always permitted to avail himself of his friend's offers to mainprise him[9].

Langland not only criticises but he suggests reforms which would bring justice within reach of all and limit the power of

> Seriauntes...that serven atte barre,
> To plede for penyes · and poundes the lawe,
> And nat for love of oure lord · unlose hure lyppes ones.
> Thow my3t bet mete the myst · on malverne hulles,
> Than gete a mom of hure mouth · til moneye be hem shewid[10].

He describes the power of the Lady Mede as being almost unlimited:

> hue doth men lese here londe · and here lyf bothe;
> Hue leteth passe prisoners · and paieth for hem ofte,
> And geveth the gailer gold · and grotes to-gederes,
> To unfetery the false · and fle where hem lyketh;
> And taketh trewe by the top · and tieth hem faste,
> And hongeth him for haterede · that harmede nevere[11].

The complaints of poor men that

> Lawe is so lordlich · and loth to maken ende[12],

1 B v 253; C vii 248.   **2** B vi 37.   **3** B iii 90.   **4** A iii 145, 178; B iii 149, 184; C iv 187, 231.   **5** A iii 209; B iii 215; C iv 273.   **6** B xx 17; C xxiii 17.   **7** A iv 75; B iv 88, xvi 264; C v 84, xix 282; *Paston Letters*, Text i, pp. 203, 204.   **8** A iv 99; B iv 112, xviii 183, cf. C xxi 189; C v 107.   **9** B ii 196; C iii 208.   **10** C i 160, cf. B p 211.   **11** C iv 173, cf. A iii 131, B iii 135.   **12** A iii 156; B iii 160; C iv 199.

convinced him that law should be a "laborere[1]," and lawyers should lower their fees, since heo beoth loth

> To mote for mene men · but ʒif thei hadde money[2].

He regrets that

> many a Justice an Juroure · wolde for Johan do more,
> Than *pro dei pietate*[3].

In order that men of law might be commanded "of the pore people no peneworth to take" he suggests that

> Of princes and prelatus · heor pencion schulde aryse[4].

Lawyers who charged no fees to the poor man were commended:

> he that spendeth his speche · and speketh for the pore
> That is innocent and neodi · and no mon hath apeyret,
> Cumforteth him in his caas · coveiteth not his goodes,
> Bote for ur lordes love · lawe for him scheweth,
> Schal no devel at his deth-day · deren him worth a myte,
> That he ne worth siker saaf[5].

But, according to Langland, they were doing no more than their duty; since human intelligence, like fire, water and air, was intended for the use of all men:

> hit is symonye, to sulle · that send is of grace;
> That is, witt and water · wynd, and fuyr the furthe,
> These foure sholden be fre · to alle folk that hit nedeth[6].

KNIGHTS, METHODS OF WARFARE

The author of *Piers Plowman* dates back the foundation of knighthood to David, who had first made men swear on their swords to obey truth for ever[7]. Commoners laboured and provided for the knight[8], in order that he might defend them and their church from "wastors and wikkede men[9]," and their crops from wild beasts and birds. The good knight's services merited a quick passage through purgatory, and a place amongst the patriarchs in paradise[10]. Unfortunately, the knights of the fourteenth century did not always fulfil the compact[11], but were often guilty of greed and discourtesy[12]. In his first revision Langland

---

1 A III 282, IV 130; B III 298, IV 147; C IV 456, V 144.   2 A VIII 45, cf. B VII 39, C X 44.   3 B VII 44, XI 217.   4 A VIII 48, cf. B VII 43.
5 A VIII 50, cf. B VII 46, C X 46.   6 C X 55, cf. A VIII 56, B VII 52.
7 A I 96; B I 102; C II 102.   8 A I 92; B I 94; C II 90.   9 A VII 30, 148; B VI 28, 161; C IX 26, 156, X 223.   10 A VIII 9; B VII 9; C X 9.
11 A IV 105.   12 A II 45; B II 57; C III 58.

cautions knights against oppressing the poor[1], and records that through their extravagance they were indebted to dishonest tradesmen, and their estates eaten up with usury[2].

Some of the picturesque customs of what is said to be one of the earliest institutions of the realm[3] are mentioned in the second version. The champion of evil is represented as a successful knight[4], unseating one opponent after the other. Christ is described in the allegory as the ideal knight[5]; and many of the knight's privileges and duties are recorded in the description of the Crucifixion. Outward signs of respect were paid to the knight by commoners[6]; and only the "kny3te with a kene spere y-grounde[7]" might joust with one who was a "kny3te and kynges sone." The knight was supposed to possess "londe... lynage riche...good loos of hus hondes[8]." Almost sacred importance was attached to the laws of chivalry. The passages describing converted Jews as franklins, freemen "and gentelmen with Jesu," prescribe a definite limit to doctrines of equality and brotherhood:

> For the best ben somme riche · and somme beggers and pore.
> For alle are we Crystes creatures · and of his coffres riche,
> And bretheren as of o blode · as wel beggares as erles[9].

The Church's democratic theories were confined within her own borders. Though Langland argued that

> Kinghod and kni3thod · for au3t I can aspie,
> Helpith nou3t to hevene · at one 3eris ende,
> Ne richesse ne rentis · ne realte of lordis[10],

we gather elsewhere that he had respect for a long line of noble ancestors. Some of the facts that he records justify his high opinion of knighthood.

Knightly courtesy was not confined to speech, and disrespectful treatment of a dead body was punished by loss of rank[11]. No knight might take advantage of another man's infirmity:

> To do the blynde bete hym ybounde · it was a boyes conseille.
> Cursed caytyve! · kni3thod was it nevere
> To mysdo a ded body · by day or by ny3te[12].

1 B III 313; C IV 471.　　**2** B V 255; C VII 250.　　**3** B P 112; C I 139.
4 B XX 122; C XXIII 123.　　**5** B XVIII; C XXI.　　**6** B XIX 28; C XXII 28.
7 B XVIII 76 ff.; C XXI 79 ff.　　**8** B XI 285; C XIV 108 ff.　　**9** B XI 191.
10 A XI 222, cf. B X 333.　　**11** B XVIII 93; C XXI 97.　　**12** B XVIII 95; C XXI 98.

According to the various descriptions of Christ in armour, the knight wore coat-armour bearing his colours and cognizance, helmet and habergeon[1]. A paltock (short coat), or, according to the later version, plate-armour, was also worn[2]. The knight was mounted in the lists, and a splendidly attired herald read the blason upon his armour and announced his titles[3]. The knight before he was dubbed had neither spurs nor spear[4]; he sought to win by his prowess "gilt spures" and "galoches y-couped," or shoes ornamented by slashing or slitting.

The few later additions to the picture of knighthood suggest that the poet was still more possessed by the fear that an age of decadence had set in. Though secular knights[5] still set the priesthood a good example of unselfish devotion[6] in their own province of battle for the truth, yet decay threatened the foundations of chivalry. New knights were chosen for their wealth, and monks and nuns purchased knight-fees for their relatives[7]. Soap-sellers and their sons became knights[8]; and, though outward display was maintained, the spirit of chivalry was lost.

Every knight shared in the defence of the realm, and in time of war he was responsible for the officers and sergeants-at-arms placed over the common soldiers. He was obliged to give account of the mercenaries he employed[9], since no man was entitled to payment unless he were registered[10]:

Kynges and knyghtes · that kepen and defenden,
Haven officers under hem · and ech of hem a certayn;
And yf thei wage men to werre · thei wryten hem in numbre;
Wol no treserour take hem wages · travayle thei nevere so sore,
Bote hii beon nempned in the numbre · of hem that ben ywaged.
Alle othere in bataille · beeth yholde brybours,
Pilours and pyke-herneys · in eche parshe a-corsede.

Rewards and high rank were awarded to the soldiers after a great victory[11].

In the heat of battle there was little scope for the customs of chivalry. First the "foregoers[12]" attempted to create confusion amongst the opposing forces. Before the minstrels tuned up or herald-at-arms announced the titles of the champions, the lord

1 B XVIII 22, XIX 12; C XXI 21, XXII 12.　　2 C XXI 24, cf. B XVIII 25.
3 B XIV 24, XVI 177, 253; C XIX 187, 271.　　4 B XVIII 13; C XXI 11.
5 C XVIII 289.　　6 C XIX 95.　　7 C VI 76.　　8 C VI 72.　　9 A III
210; B III 216, cf. C IV 274; B XIX 335; C XXII 341.　　10 Cf. B XX 256,
C XXIII 257.　　11 C IV 248.　　12 B XX 80; C XXIII 81.

in command raised his war-cry and his standard was borne into the field by a chosen knight[1]. The successful warrior unseated one enemy after the other with such a cry as "Alarme! alarme!... eche lyf kepe his owene!"

Baselard (or short sword), broad-sword, lance, axe and hatchet were the usual weapons of knights[2]. Some of the lower ranks fought with bow and feathered or broad-hooked arrows[3]. Long knives[4] were favourite weapons and some men armed themselves with quickly-improvised slings[5]. These primitive weapons made armour and high walls a safe protection[6]. An army, whose progress was hindered by non-combatants, or inferior in arms and discipline[7], usually retreated to cover. An attempt was made to secure the position by surrounding it with a moat until it bore some resemblance to a fort[8].

An elaborate system of defence had been perfected by the fourteenth century. At the first news of the invader's approach the castle gate was made fast with iron bars and chains[9]. "Bowes of brake," or crossbows worked with a crank or handle, held the foe at a distance for some time. If the enemy reached the walls, boiling substances were poured down and heavy stones hurled from machines known as "mangonels." The ground over which the attacking force[10] was obliged to bring up its war material had been previously prepared with deadly four-spiked balls or "calthrops." Scaling-ladders were thrown down by hooks[11]. "Brazen guns," pouring out shot upon the attackers, foreshadowed the time when gunpowder would render the splendid medieval castles insecure.

The sufferings of an army invading a foreign land were not confined to the toil of battle and ministrations of the unskilled leech[12]. An improvident marshal might expose them to hunger and neglect until they were obliged to give up the campaign[13]. Such had been the condition of Edward III's army in their last invasion of Normandy, when an intensely cold winter had completed the demoralisation of the English force[14].

---

1 B xv 428, xx 68, 90; C xxiii 69, 91.   2 B iii 303; C iv 461.
3 B xx 116, 224; C xxiii 117, 225.   4 B xx 218; C xxiii 219.
5 B xx 162, 216; C xxiii 163, 217.   6 B i 156; C ii 155.   7 B xix
355; C xxii 361.   8 B xix 359; C xxii 365.   9 C xxi 283.   10 B xviii
250; C xxi 263.   11 C xxi 296.   12 B xx 303; C xxiii 305.
13 A iii 194; B iii 200; C iv 258, 259.   14 A iii 182; B iii 188.

III

COUNTRY LIFE

The Landowner and his Household

E VEN in times of peace the system of "maintenance" encouraged the lord to provide for a "riche retynaunce[1],"
including paid servants[2] eager for money[3]. Foregoers attended
him when he rode from manor to manor on his palfrey, followed
by a pack of hounds[4]. On state occasions he was surrounded
by young men, either mounted or running on foot[5]; since

> Emperours and erles · and alle manere lordes
> Thoruh ʒiftes haven ʒemen · to rennen and to ryde[6].

The higher nobility and clergy[7] imitated the royal custom of
maintaining minstrels, sometimes attached to their households[8].

At the head of the household was the steward who was expected "to sitten and demen[9]." He guarded his lord's rights
by taking charge of food and clothing[10], possibly by preventing
such servants as the "redyng-king" from spending too much of
their time in the tavern[11], and by supervising the entertainment
of the numerous guests. A cleric might discharge the duties of
steward[12] or seneschal[13] in a noble household. The paneter, or
keeper of the pantry[14], is the only indoor servant mentioned in
Piers Plowman.

A typical manor-house was surrounded with a moat spanned
by a permanent bridge raised on piers[15]; the walls were provided with battlements and parapet, and halls and chambers
were covered by a leaden roof. The gates were barred and the
hinges hung on hooks[16]. At each postern there was a porter or

---

1 A ii 35; B ii 53; C iii 55.   2 A iii 210; B iii 216, cf. C iv 274.
3 B xiv 142.   4 A ii 162; B ii 60, 187; C iii 61, 198.   5 B x 309, 316;
C vi 161, 168.   6 C iv 270, cf. A iii 206, B iii 212.   7 B xiii 437;
C viii 97.   8 A xi 33; B x 46.   9 A v 39; B P 96, v 48; C i 94,
vi 146.   10 B xix 251; C xxii 256.   11 A v 166; B v 323; C vii 372.
12 B P 96; C i 94.   13 C i 93.   14 C xvii 151.   15 A vi 76;
B v 595; C viii 233.   16 B xx 296; C xxiii 298.

"gateward" who enquired the name and business of all comers before opening the wicket[1]. Undesirable persons, for whom no one within the castle walls would be responsible, were turned away[2]; but all other travellers were entertained according to their rank. Their host gave a hearty welcome to his friends and equals, and they "wisshen and wypeden and wenten to the dyner[3]," which was served to them on the daïs in the hall. Other guests were received and "yput to be mettes[4]" at the side-tables by the steward of the hall[5]. The pilgrim, palmer, or "pore heremyte[6]" lingered outside and cried:

> for Cristes love of hevene.
> A meles mete for a poure man · other moneye[7],

until the host called him in with rough courtesy,

> Welcome, wye, go and wasshe · thow shalt sitte sone[8].

Beggars sat on the ground with

> mete more than ynough · ac nou3t so moche worship
> As tho that seten atte syde-table · or with the sovereignes of the halle[9].

Others cried at the gate until the meal was ended and the tables were removed[10]. Within, during the feast, musicians played and implored "a largesse[11]" and, when they were silent, voices were raised in dispute[12] or the guests contributed "a fitte" as the harp was passed along[13].

Sometimes this open-handed hospitality seems to have been the occasion of permanent injury to the estate. If the master-friar, received "for the moste worthy[14]," found great favour with his host, the lawful heir might, at the lord's death[15], discover that he had been disinherited in favour of the mendicants[16]. Langland, however, agreed that it was the duty of wealthy landlords to entertain travellers, including minstrels:

> alle manere mynstrales · men wot wel the sothe,
> To under-fonge hem faire · by-falleth for the ryche,
> For the lordes love and ladies · that thei with lengen[17].

1 A vi 85, 92, 108; B v 604, 611, cf. C viii 249; B v 628, xx 329; C viii 243, 271, xxiii 331; "Etin the Forester," p. 127, verse 22.   **2** A vi 115; B v 636, xx 340; C viii 280, xxiii 342.   **3** B xiii 27; C xvi 31; Froissart, Globe Edition, p. 386, ii cliii.   **4** B xiii 35; C xvi 41.   **5** C xvi 40.   **6** B xiii 29; C xvi 33.   **7** C xvi 35.   **8** B xiii 32.   **9** B xii 199, cf. C xv 139.   **10** C ix 285.   **11** B xiii 449; C viii 109.   **12** A xi 39; B x 52; C xii 35.   **13** A i 137.   **14** B xiii 33; C xvi 39.   **15** B x 312; C vi 164.   **16** B xv 316; C xviii 55.   **17** C x 128.

He regretted, however, that such men were specially welcome on account of their immoral tales and flattery when other dependents were neglected[1]. Lords who spent much in entertainment did not necessarily escape the charge of meanness[2]:

> Ne were mercy in mene men · more than in riche,
> Mendinantz meteles · mi3te go to bedde[3].

At the time Langland was writing, the old sociable practices were becoming less usual. Private chamber and chimney corner were beginning to attract the lord and lady from the hall. Langland regrets this:

> Elyng is the halle · uche daye in the wyke,
> There the lorde ne the lady · liketh nou3te to sytte.
> Now hath uche riche a reule · to eten bi hym-selve
> In a pryve parloure · for pore mennes sake,
> Or in a chambre with a chymneye · and leve the chief halle,
> That was made for meles · men to eten inne;
> And al to spare to spille · that spende shal an other[4].

METHODS OF AGRICULTURE

The lord derived his income from an estate consisting of numerous manors scattered over the country; and in spite of the frequent progresses the owner made from manor to manor, often consuming the year's produce of one before passing on to another, he was seldom able to supervise his servants and tenants in person[5]. He was obliged to rely on his steward, who collected rents and information from servants permanently residing on each manor. This process is best described by the land-owner:

> Thanne lough there a lorde · and "by this li3te," sayde,
> "I halde it ry3te and resoun · of my reve to take
> Al that myne auditour · or elles my stuwarde
> Conseilleth me by her acounte · and my clerkes wrytynge.
> With *spiritus intellectus* · they seke the reves rolls,
> And with *spiritus fortitudinis* · feeche it I wole[6]."

The reeve was responsible for the behaviour of labourers and the cultivation of the estate, and the "reeve-rolls," or detailed

---

1 A vii 48; B vi 54; C ix 50.   2 C xii 28, cf. B x 30.   3 A xi 51; B x 64, cf. C xii 49.   4 B x 94.   5 Cf. methods of Earl Gaston of Foix as related by Froissart (Globe edn, Berner's translation, p. 330, vol. ii, chap. 26).   6 B xix 456; C xxii 461.

accounts of the property, were kept by him or his clerks. In spite of all precautions much depended on his character and ability:

> An unredy reve · thi residue shal spene,
> That menye moththe was maister ynne · in a mynte-while;
> Up-holderes on the hul · shullen have hit to selle[1].

"Rondulf the reve · of Rotelondes sokene[2]" is mentioned as being an undesirable character; and the poet reproves the reeve and his clerks for performing their duties less creditably than humbler members of the household[3].

Labour was provided by the villeins or bondmen[4], who received houses and strips of land to cultivate for themselves, in return for their services[5]. According to strict law, they were almost slaves without legal rights, and might neither make charters nor sell property without their lord's permission[6]:

> For may no cherl a chartre make · ne hus catel selle
> With-oute leve of the lorde · no lawe wolde hit graunte.
> Ac he may renne in arerage · and rome.fro home
> As a recheles caitif · other reneyed, as hit semeth[7].

By leaving the estate without permission, to escape from his creditors, the churl seldom improved his condition.

Social distinctions[8] lingered longest in rural districts; and the three classes of society, priest, knight and labourer, were still distinct there:

> For holy churche hoteth · alle manere puple
> Under obedience to bee · and buxum to the lawe.
> Furst, religious, of religion · here ruele to holde,
> And under obedience to be · by dayes and by nyghtes;
> Lewede men to laborie; · and lordes to honte
> In frythes and in forestes · for fox and other bestes
> That in wilde wodes ben · and in wast places,
> As wolves that wyryeth men · wommen and children[9].

Matters of the estate were settled at the "knight's court[10]," and the landlord seems to have ordered the "love days," or days of arbitration[11]. Hence the advice to refuse gifts; and again

> mis-beode thou not thi bonde-men · the beter thou schalt spede,
> And that thi-self be trewe of tonge · and tales thou hate,
> Bote hit beo wisdam or wit · thi werkmen to chaste[12].

1 C xiii 216.   **2** A ii 78; B ii 110; C iii 112.   **3** B x 469; C xii 297. **4** C vi 62.   **5** C x 223.   **6** A p 96; B p 216; C i 219, vi 65.   **7** C xiii 61, cf. B xi 122.   **8** Langlois, *Moralistes*, 80; "La Bible au Seigneur de Berzé"; Wyclif, iii 206, Tract xv, "A Schort Reule of Lif." **9** C x 219.   **10** C viii 33.   **11** A iii 154, xi 20; B iii 157, v 427, x 20, 307; C iv 196, vi 159, xii 17.   **12** A vii 45, cf. B vi 46, C ix 42.

The alms of lords and ladies who disregarded this counsel were said to be unworthy of the Church's acceptance[1]. Patience was the serf's only comfort when faced by "gyves," "grete lordes wrath" and "prisone[2]." There are indications that the landlord's power was waning; for casual labourers refused the old wages and demanded better food[3]. It was also sometimes possible to escape from bondage by taking clerical orders[4]. But Langland, like all his contemporaries, admitted the justice of serfdom[5]; the freeman naturally became a thrall as a result of his own misconduct or of the fortunes of war[6]:

> To be called a kni3te is faire · for men shal knele to hym;
> To be called a kynge is fairer · for he may kny3tes make;
> Ac to be conquerour called · that cometh of special grace,
> And of hardynesse of herte · and of hendenesse bothe,
> To make lordes of laddes · of londe that he wynneth,
> And fre men foule thralles · that folweth nou3t his lawes.
> The Juwes, that were gentil-men · Jesu thei dispised,
> Bothe his lore and his lawe · now ar thei lowe cherlis.
> As · wyde as the worlde is · wonyeth there none
> But under tribut and taillage · as tykes and cherles.
> And tho that bicome Crysten · by conseille of the baptiste,
> Aren frankeleynes, fre men · thorw fullyng that thei toke,
> And gentel-men with Jesu · for Jesus was yfulled,
> And uppon Calvarye on crosse · ycrouned kynge of Jewes[7].

Many details of medieval methods of agriculture are preserved in *Piers Plowman* and the poet seems to have been personally acquainted with this industry; though the dreamer gave the impression that he, a clerk, knew nothing of manual work[8]. Langland insists on the primary importance of the work, which gave employment to by far the greater part of the population[9]. He spoke of it as the ideal occupation; and the chief figure of the first part of the poem is the ploughman, afterwards identified with Christ[10]. Implements were primitive. The plough was drawn by oxen and had a plough-foot, to clear out the furrows[11]. "Dykers" and "delvers" saw to the ditches and balks:

> Now is Perkyn and his pilgrymes · to the plowe faren;
> To erie this halve-acre · holpyn hym manye.

1 B xv 304; C xviii 44.   **2** B xiv 51; C xvi 254.   **3** A vii 295; B vi 309; C ix 331.   **4** C vi 70.   **5** B xviii 103; C xxi 108. **6** B xx 145; C xxiii 146.   **7** B xix 28, cf. C xxii 28.   **8** C vi 22. **9** A P 20; B P 20, 119, iii 307; C i 22, 145, iv 465, etc.   **10** A vi 28; B v 544; C viii 182.   **11** A vii 96; B v 105, vi 193, xix 257; C xxii 262.

Dikeres and delveres · digged up the balkes;
There-with was Perkyn apayed · and preysed hem faste.
Other werkeman there were · that wrou3ten ful 3erne,
Eche man in his manere · made hym-self to done,
And some to plese Perkyn · piked up the wedes[1].

When Piers is preparing to sow he says he will "cast" on him

my clothes · yclouted and hole,
My cokeres and my coffes · for colde of my nailles,
And hange myn hoper at myn hals · in stede of a scrippe;
A busshel of bredcorne · brynge me ther-inne[2].

Langland says that, after the pestilence, sowers could not esti-
mate the value of the crop by the seed sown[3]. Growing weeds
were destroyed by harrowing[4]; and when the corn was in ear[5],
it was guarded day and night. Wild animals and crows were
frightened away and nets were laid to catch birds[6]. The hayward with his horn challenged foot-passengers and watched for
thieves[7]. When the harvest was finished the crops were threshed
with flails in the barns in which they were stored[8].

If a farm-hand were required he was probably questioned as
Reason questioned the dreamer:

"Canstow serven," he seide · "other syngen in a churche,
Other coke for my cokers · other to the cart picche,
Mowe other mowen · other make bond to sheves,
Repe other be a repereyve · and a-ryse erliche,
Other have an horne and be haywarde · and liggen oute a nyghtes,
And kepe my corn in my croft · fro pykers and theeves?
Other shappe shon other clothes · other shep other kyn kepe,
Heggen other harwen · other swyn other gees dryve,
Other eny other kyns craft · that to the comune nedeth,
Hem that bedreden be · by-lyve to fynde[9]?"

Sheep-farming was important; and Langland refers to remedies
used against diseases which spoiled the wool[10]. The shepherd's
knowledge of stars and winds, too, seems to have been almost
proverbial[11]. Swine, geese and cattle[12] were watched; for the
small farmer counted among his enemies, thieves, outlaws and
his more powerful neighbours. The latter (perhaps pretending
to act as royal purveyors) did much damage to his property.

1 B vi 107, cf. A vii 98; C ix 112.　　　2 B vi 61, cf. A vii 55;
C ix 58.　　　3 B xv 357; C xviii 100.　　　4 B xix 306; C vi 19,
xxii 311.　　　5 C vi 16.　　　6 A v 199, vii 129; B v 355; C vii 406.
7 C vii 368, xiv 47.　　8 A vii 173; B vi 186; C ix 179, 199.　　9 C vi 12.
10 C x 262.　　　11 B xv 354; C xviii 98.　　　12 A vii 129, 184, 274;
B vi 142, 289; C ix 312.

In the allegory Peace complains of Wrong in a bill addressed to Parliament:

> Bothe my gees and my grys · his gadelynges feccheth;
> I dar nouȝte for fere of hym · fyȝte ne chyde.
> He borwed of me bayard · he brouȝte hym home nevre,
> Ne no ferthynge ther-fore · for nauȝte I couthe plede.
> He meyneteneth his men · to morther myne hewen,
> Forstalleth my feyres · and fiȝteth in my chepynge,
> And breketh up my bernes dore · and bereth aweye my whete,
> And taketh me but a taile · for ten quarteres of otes[1].

Maintenance protected the stronger party; it was not remarkable that the farmer coveted his neighbour's cattle and, profiting by the absence of hedges, encroached on his neighbour's furrows and reaped what he had not sown[2].

In dry weather the cart and mare were used to carry manure, and dykes were made[3]. Barns were built of timber and wattle and overlaid with mortar[4]. Thatching and whittling pegs occupied the men's spare time while the women spun or wove[5]. From the questions addressed to the would-be labourer, it appears that country labourers sometimes made their own clothes and shoes[6].

Langland[7] mentions cheese and oaten cakes as the farm labourer's staple diet; but the quality of his food varied with season and harvest. After a good harvest, penny-ale bacon and cabbage a day-old[8] were scorned, and new corn, wheaten bread, fresh meat and fish were required[9]. In hard times the labourer was obliged to exist until the next harvest on bread made from peas and beans, bran, pottage, porridge, various kinds of fruit and vegetable, and a little cream and curds[10]:

> "I have no peny," quod Pers · "poletes to bugge,
> Nouther gees ne grys · bote twey grene cheeses,
> And a fewe cruddes and craym · and a therf cake,
> And a lof of benes and bren · i-bake for my children.
> And I sigge, bi my soule · I have no salt bacon,
> Ne no cokeneyes, bi Crist · colopus to maken.
> Bot I have porettes and percyl · and moni colplontes,

1 B IV 51, cf. A IV 38, C V 49.   2 B XIII 364; C VII 262.   3 A VII 274; B III 308, VI 289; C IX 184, 198, 312.   4 B VI 144, XIX 315; C XXII 320.   5 B III 308; C IV 466, IX 199.   6 C VI 18.   7 A VII 268; B VI 283; C IX 305.   8 A VII 295; B VI 309; C IX 331.   9 A VII 291; B VI 305, VII 120; C IX 327.   10 A VII 171, 176, 279, 291; B VI 184, 189, 294, 305; C IX 182, 317, 327; "Lizie Lindsay," verse 16.

And eke a cou, and a calf · and a cart-mare
To drawe a-feld my donge · whil the drouhthe lasteth.
Bi this lyflode I mot lyven · til Lammasse tyme;
Bi that, ich hope forte have · hervest in my croft;
Thenne may I dihte thi dyner · as the deore lyketh[1]."

The plenty of harvest usually attracted a number of idlers[2]
who hoped for

no dede to do · bote drynke and to slepe[3];

though the farmer required hard workers[4] and reserved for those
who had ploughed the right of gleaning[5]. A few months' good
living prepared the way for sickness[6]; and after a bad harvest,
followed by famine and pestilence, many folk died[7].

1 A VII 267, cf. B VI 282, C IX 304.   2 A VII 173, 290; B VI 186, 193,
304; C IX 179, 186, 326.   3 C VI 9.   4 A VII 61, 107; B VI 116; C IX 121.
5 B VI 68; C IX 67.   6 A VII 244; B VI 259; C IX 271.   7 B VI 331,
XIII 269, 404; C VII 430, IX 354.

IV

TOWN LIFE

Officers

IN the fourteenth century the privilege of dwelling within town-walls was much valued; if only because personal safety did not there depend entirely on a man's ability in smiting "bothe with ston and with staf[1]." Traders were prosperous[2]; and, according to *Piers Plowman*, their interests were narrow. Towards the class beneath them they seem to have behaved haughtily, like some mendicants,

> ful proude-herted men · paciente of tonge,
> And boxome as of berynge · to burgeys and to lordes,
> And to pore peple · han peper in the nose[3].

Their wealth enabled them to surround themselves with what they considered luxuries[4]; but they and their wives seem to have watched each other jealously and resented any individual display of success[5].

Formerly every precaution had been taken to award the freedom of the city only to persons who had served the citizens faithfully; but in Langland's day unscrupulous retailers and even usurers had by bribery won a place amongst the freemen[6]. Langland seems to use the word *franklin* loosely; partly as a mere synonym of *freeman* (as it first doubtless had been), and partly in Chaucer's sense[7]. He uses "*Frenchemen*" curiously as a synonym for *franklins*. In one passage[8] he describes "Frenchemen" and freemen as having their children taught to speak French. Their children had always been considered worthy of being admitted to holy orders[9], and the franklin's son, in the ordinary course of events, inherited his father's privileges and property[10].

Upon the burgesses depended the prosperity of the com-

---

1 C vii 106.　　2 A P 31; B P 31; C I 33.　　　3 B xv 195.
4 A iii 150; B iii 162; C iv 201.　　5 B v 129, xii 148; C vii 96,146,
xv 91.　　6 C iv 108.　　7 B xix 39; C xxii 39.　　8 B xi 375.
9 C vi 64.　　10 C xi 240.

munity. Individual interests were supposed to be subordinated
to the common good; and there was no place for those who

wilnen and wolde · as best were for hem-selve,
Thauh the kyng and the comune · al the cost hadde[1].

Even the penances imposed by the Church were turned to
common profit; for the townsmen, besides endowing religious
bodies, after the manner of noblemen, founded secular schools,
hospitals and funds for the relief of helpless persons, and contributed to the upkeep of roads and bridges[2].

The mayor ruled as royal deputy within the town walls[3]. He
was responsible to the king for the townsfolk's behaviour and
acted as an intermediary between king and commons[4]; so that
only the half-witted wanderer passed him in the street without
respectfully saluting him[5]. The wise ploughman advised his son
to accept his decisions, whatever he might think of his actions:

Maistres, as the meyres ben · and grete men senatours,
What thei comaunde as by the kyng · contrepleide hit nevere,
Al that they hoten, ich hote · heyliche, thow suffre hem;
By here warnyng and worchyng · worch thow ther-after;
. . . .
Ac after here doynge do thow nat · my dere sone[6].

As state matters were dated by the sovereign's reign, so were
municipal matters by that of the mayor; as "whan Chichestre
was maire[7]." Though the mayor was respected as a man of
property, he was possibly not proof against bribes of silver and
ruby rings[8]. He had been known to add new and unauthorized
names to the freemen's roll, favouring wealthy rather than
honourable candidates[9]. The poet passes over the aldermen with
a brief mention and has little to say of bailiffs and beadles[10],
but some personal grievance seems to have accounted for the
insertion of "Bette the budele of Banneburies sokne[11]" who
occupies in the last version the place of the "bedel of Bockyng-
ham-shire." Another town official, the scavenger[12], is said to
have been present with his mate among the tavern company.

1 C iv 387.   2 A viii 28; B vii 26; C x 30.   3 B i 158; C ii 157.
4 A iii 67; B iii 76, cf. C iv 77.   5 C x 122.   6 C ix 87.   7 B xiii
271.   8 A viii 171; B vii 184, xiv 288; C x 335, xvii 126.   9 A iii
78; B iii 87; C iv 77, 108, 115.   10 A iii 2; B iii 2; C iv 2, v 188.
11 C iii 111, cf. A ii 77, B ii 109.   12 C vii 371, cf. A v 165; B v 322.

CRAFTSMEN AND TRADERS

There is no direct mention in *Piers Plowman* of the guilds which in each town controlled and developed the various crafts and trades; but the conditions under which trade was carried on are described. There seems to have been a certain amount of hostility between tradesmen on the one hand and artisans on the other. The price, quality and place of sale of food-stuffs and materials were regulated, rather for the benefit of the community than for the merchant's convenience; and the traders retaliated by practising numerous frauds on the public, much to the indignation of contemporary moralists[1]. Specially appointed officials collected the tolls from merchants who made use of the market or fair[2], and recognised brokers were registered on the city rolls[3]. But a broker would sometimes evade the regulations and under-value his neighbour's goods, if he could profit in so doing[4].

The merchants usually appear in *Piers Plowman* as public enemies, skilled in lying[5] and in cheating their customers by using false weights and unsealed measures or by misusing the measures sealed and approved by the local authorities[6].

One who was the "plight prentys" of "Symme atte noke" confesses that, learning the "donet," or primer, of trade,

Furst I leornede to lyȝe · a lessun or tweyne,
And wikkedliche for to weie · was myn other lessun[7].

The trader profited by "forestalling" the ordinary purchases and "regrating," or reselling, the goods at a large profit[8].

"Brewesters, bakers, bochers and cookes[9]" bought tenements and built high houses with their illegal profits. The commons regarded them as the "men uppon molde that most harm worchen" and attributed the "sondry sorwes in cytees[10]," such as fevers, fires and floods, to divine displeasure aroused by their conduct. Some satisfaction was felt by the commons in reflect-

---

1 C IV 87.   **2** B P 220; C XIV 51.   **3** B II 65, V 130; C III 66, VII 95;
Liber Albus, I, Book III, 315; IV 586.   **4** B II 59, V 248; C III 60;
English Gilds, Toulmin Smith, p. 343, Berwick-on-Tweed, Ordinance (27).
5 A II 188; B II 212; C III 222.   **6** A V 131; B V 217, XIII 359, XIV 292;
C VII 223, 230, XVII 130; *Liber Albus*, III 2, 263, 265.   **7** A V 117,
cf. B V 203, C VII 209.   **8** A IV 43; B IV 56; C V 59; *English Gilds*,
p. 345, Toulmin Smith, Berwick-on-Tweed, Ordinance (40).   **9** A III 70.
cf. B III 79, C IV 80.   **10** C IV 90.

ing that in purgatory the merchants would be called to account
for neglecting the holy-days and swearing

> by here saule · and "so god me mote helpe!"
> A3ens clene conscience · for covetyse of wynnynge[1].

Meanwhile they remarked how frequent fires were:

> som tyme thorw a brewere
> Meny burgagys ben ybrent · and bodyes ther-ynne;
> And thorw a candel, clomyng · in a corsed place,
> Fel a-doun, and for-brende · forth al the rewe[2].

The system of bartering in open markets and displaying mer-
chandise on stalls before the shops[3] encouraged each man to
advertise his goods loudly. He arranged them to hide all de-
ficiencies[4], and sometimes produced false witnesses to support
him and confuse the buyer[5]. If one man succeeded in selling his
wares quickly[6], his rival decried them and called attention to
the superior value of his own. Salutations[7] in the market-place
failed to cloak the bitterness of enemies who had struck hard
bargains with each other[8]. The Church was advised by the poet
to refuse tithes from these men[9], who sometimes added usury
to their other sins[10].

Thrift and cunning were therefore great assets to a trader,
and were usually well-developed during the years in which a
boy served as "plight prentys[11]" and gained the right to practise
a special craft or trade[12]. Skilled craftsmen were paid by their
masters[13]; but the 'prentice sometimes gave a considerable sum
of money for his training[14]. He wore a special dress, and his
education was confined to acquiring practical experience[15]. A
prosperous merchant from the "ferthest ende of Norfolke[16]" was
represented in the poem as being unacquainted with the meaning
of the word "restitution"; it was not in his line.

The high prices at which the commons grumbled were partly
occasioned by difficulties of transport. Business was usually
transacted at fairs held periodically in thickly populated dis-

---

1 A VIII 22; B VII 20; C X 24. 2 C IV 104. 3 A P 104; B P 225;
C I 226. 4 B XIII 362; C VII 260. 5 B XIII 359; Wyclif, *Pauper
Rusticus*, VIIth Commandment. 6 B V 129; C VII 95. 7 A V 83;
B V 92, 100. 8 B XV 160. 9 B XV 83, 105; C VII 300, XVIII 46.
10 B XIX 346; C XXII 352. 11 A V 116; B V 202; C VII 208. 12 *Liber
Albus*, III, Part 2, 272. 13 A III 218; B III 224; C IV 281. 14 B V 256;
C VII 251. 15 A II 190; B II 214; C III 224. 16 B V 239.

tricts of England or on the continent. Great fairs were held at St Giles's Down, Weyhill and Winchester[1]. English 'prentices and servants crossed the sea to Bruges and travelled as far as Prussia[2]; though the traveller was obliged in these times to face many discomforts and real danger. Owing to the bad condition of the roads, long journeys were usually made on horseback or even on foot along the routes shown by the foresters[3]. Special messengers, on showing the letters they bore[4], were privileged to pass the length and breadth of England without hindrance[5], but the merchant[6], when conveying his goods on pack-horses from town to town, was obliged to journey slowly. Local authorities levied tolls[7] and obliged the merchant to carry his credentials with him[8]. The hayward who had permitted the messenger to pass quickly through his wheat-field required pledges or indemnities from other travellers:

> Other hus hatt other hus hode · othere elles hus gloves
> The marchaunt mot for-go · other moneye of hus porse.

An armed guard was the only protection against highwaymen who haunted such places as the approach to St Giles's Down[9]. The hosteler seems to have been the one friend of travellers[10]; he was proverbially a genial man, willing to oblige his guests in any way[11].

Poor packmen could not pay for protection when travelling about in search of a market for their goods[12]. Rose, the dish-seller[13], or Hugh, the needle-seller[14], might lose their entire stock-in-trade during a night's rest. The pedlar's poverty was supposed to drive him to catching and killing cats "for coveitise of here skynnes[15]."

Certain tradesmen, notably the miller and the brewer, had no need to travel far from home and were represented in every parish. "Munde the miller[16]" is only mentioned in *Piers Plowman* as a lover of wealth and an ignorant fellow who did not recognise the somewhat obscure phrase "*multa fecit Deus*[17]." The trade of brewing and selling beer was carried on by many of the persons

1 A v 119; B v 205; C v 51, VII 211. 2 B XIII 392; C VII 278. 3 B XVII 112. 4 A II 203; B II 227; C III 237. 5 A IV 115; B IV 132; C v 129. 6 C XIV 56. 7 C XIV 51. 8 C XIV 38. 9 C v 51. 10 A v 172. 11 B XVII 73, 115; C XX 74. 12 B v 233; C VII 235. 13 A v 166; B v 323; C VII 372. 14 A v 161; B v 318; C VII 365. 15 B v 258. 16 A II 80; B II 111; C III 113. 17 B X 44.

mentioned in the poem[1]. No licence was necessary and the beer-seller briefly disposed of the endless regulations securing good beer for the public:

"ȝe, bawe!" quath a brewere · "ich wol nat beo rueled[2]."

A craftsman[3] brought home barley so that his wife, "Rose the regratour," might brew beer and spend part of her time in "hockerye," but Beton the brewster gave her whole time to keeping her tavern[4].

There were many varieties, from penny-ale[5], or even half-penny-ale[6], to "podyng ale," or thick ale. The very best brown ale was carefully stowed away in the bedchamber[7]. All kinds of ale were supposed to comply with regulations, but the ale-seller seems usually to have outwitted the ale-conner and defrauded the public[8]. A cheap kind of perry known as "piri-whit[9]" was mixed with the ale; and thick and thin ale were sold together[10]. Dregs and refuse were palmed off as good liquor, and all qualities were drawn from the same tap[11]. Though the use of "sealed measures" was strictly enforced, some ale-sellers continued to measure their gallons by drinking-cups, to their own advantage[12]. Hot spiced drinks[13], seasoned with pepper, peony seeds, garlic and fennel were sold by beer-vendors, but it is stated in the introduction to the *Liber Albus* that the keeper of the wine tavern was probably prohibited from selling ale. This would account for the tavern-keepers[14] in the "Field Full of Folk" not mentioning ale when they offered various beverages:

White wyn of Oseye · and red wyn of Gascoigne,
Of the Ryne and of the Rochel · the roste to defye.

The poet did not approve of the contemporary custom of wasting much time every day, and even on fast-days, in the ale-houses[15]. The varied company who gathered there amused themselves by jesting, quarrelling, gossiping, singing refrains and

1 C x 189; *Liber Albus*, Book 3, Pt 2, 266, Introduction, lx.   **2** C xxii 398, cf. B xix 394.   **3** A v 133; B v 219; C vii 225.   **4** A v 148; B v 306; C vii 353.   **5** A v 134, vii 297; B v 220, vi 311, xv 310; C vii 226, ix 333.   **6** A vii 293; B vi 307; C ix 329.   **7** A v 136, vii 294; B v 222, vi 308; C vii 228, ix 330.   **8** A iii 70; B iii 79; C iv 80.   **9** A v 134.   **10** B v 220; C vii 226.   **11** B xix 397; C xxii 401; Chester Play, xvii, Christ's Descent into Hell, ll. 289–292.   **12** A v 139; B v 225; C vii 231; *Liber Albus*, Introduction, lxiii.   **13** A v 155; B v 312; C vii 359; *Liber Albus*, Introduction, lxi.   **14** A p 107; B p 228; C i 229.   **15** B ii 93, 95; C iii 98, 100.

playing games which required little skill or intelligence and provided opportunity for more drinking[1].

The quality of bread was also standardised, and regulations governed the sale of all varieties from the finest "wastell bread[2]" to the bread sold for horses[3]. Bread-sellers, however, managed to evade the law and make excessive profits. The waferer, or cake-maker, mentioned in *Piers Plowman*, says that he wanders abroad to "serve many lordes[4]," and though he does not receive valuable presents and fine clothes, he yet considers himself an important member of society. Another waferer, whose comrades are a cut-purse and an apeward, is probably a more usual type[5]. Stratford seems to have been the headquarters of the bread-makers who supplied "alle Londoun," as Haukyn the waferer says:

it is nou3t longe ypassed,
There was a carful comune · whan no carte come to toune
With bake bred fro Stretforth · tho gan beggeres wepe,
And werkmen were agaste a litel · this wil be thou3te longe.
In the date of owre dry3te · in a drye Apprile,
A thousande and thre hondreth · tweis thretty and ten,
My wafres there were gesen · whan Chichestre was maire[6].

In the "Field Full of Folk" cries of "hote pies, gode gris and gees[7]" bade the crowd "gowe dine" on the food and drink for which Langland says excessive prices were often charged by butchers, cooks, brewers and brewsters[8]. The garlic-sellers assembled on the "Garleke hithe" to sell their spices[9].

Sellers of cloth shared the unpopularity of food-sellers amongst the workmen; for 'prentices to drapers, mercers and clothiers were taught to make the most of the cloth. A piece of rich "raycloth" could be stretched out from ten or twelve yards to thirteen by piercing it with a packing-needle, fastening the edges together and pressing it[10]. The illegal profits of this trade fell to the share of the employer. The spinsters were paid for spinning out the woollen yarn according to piece-work[11]; and their mistress weighed the stuff they brought her with a heavy weight.

1 A v 148, 190, vii 108; B v 306, 345, vi 117; C vii 353, 396, ix 122.
2 B v 293; C vii 341; *Liber Albus*, Introduction, lxv; iii, Part 3, 356. 3 B xiii 243; Riley, *Memorials of London*, pp. 71, 121. 4 B xiii 226; C xvi 199; *Edward I, Wardrobe Account*, p. 314. 5 A vi 120; B v 641; C viii 285.
6 B xiii 264. 7 A p 104; B p 225; C i 226. 8 A iii 70; B iii 79; C iv 80; A p 98; B p 218; C i 221. 9 A v 167; B v 324; C vii 373. 10 A v 123; B v 209; C vii 215. 11 A v 131; B v 217; C vii 223.

Though there were male weavers and tailors[1], much of the cloth seems to have been produced by female labour. Langland mentions "wollewebsteres," "weveres of lynnen" and "spin-sters[2]"; and the "shappesters sheres[3]" belonged to a female cutter.

"Cloth that cometh fro the wevyng·is nouȝt comly to were[4]"; and the medieval fuller prepared the weft for the "tailloures hande." He cleansed the cloth by treading it under water (hence his name of *walker*) or by washing it in what was probably a frame, known as the "fulling-stock." The material was then stretched on tenter hooks and fulled or tucked, a process from which the fuller took his alternative title of "tokker[5]." After-wards the cloth was scratched with rough teasel-heads to im-prove the surface. Worn garments were cleansed by scraping off the mud, washing and wringing them[6]. Then, apparently, they were well beaten and soaked in lye until the original colour was restored. Finally they were re-dyed in grain to ensure the duration of the work.

Sesse, the woman-cobbler[7], and Clement the shoe-maker[8] also frequented Beton's tavern. The cobbler of Southwark sold charms[9]. The only other mention of cobblers classed them amongst the hard-working craftsmen who met with the poet's approval[10].

Many other craftsmen are referred to in *Piers Plowman*; but no details of their lives are given. Tanners[11] appear in the "Field Full of Folk" together with miners and masons[12], whose knowledge of line and level was commented upon[13]. Their skill is used by the poet to illustrate the wonders of nature[14]; for in spite of their instruments[15], no mason could construct a "mould" or working-pattern for a magpie's nest. Like carpenters and carvers, the masons owed their craft to praiseworthy industry. The tinker and his two boys are present at the tavern and in the "Field Full of Folk[16]." Robin the Roper[17] is the umpire in the game of " New

1 A xi 18, 181; B v 554, x 18; C x 204, xii 15. 2 A p 99, v 130; B p 219, v 216; C i 222, vii 222. 3 B xiii 331; C vii 75. 4 B xv 444. 5 A p 100. 6 B xiv 18. 7 B v 315, cf. A v 158, C vii 362. 8 A v 170; B v 327; C vii 376. 9 B xiii 340; C vii 83. 10 A xi 181. 11 A p 100; C i 223. 12 A p 101; B p 221. 13 A xi 134; B x 178; C xii 126. 14 B xi 341; C xiv 161. 15 A xi 134; B x 178; C xii 126. 16 A v 160; B p 220, v 317; C vii 364. 17 A v 180; B v 336; C vii 387.

Fair." "Griffyn the Walish[1]" (or Welshman), a hackney-man, or horse-dealer, a rat-catcher and bald tooth-drawers are also present there[2].

The existence of crafts and trades is attributed to the wisdom of the commons, acting under the guidance of natural intelligence[3]; keen sight was needed by all who practised them, and no man was justified in using his skill for evil purposes[4]. In the poet's ideal land, a death penalty awaited the smith who forged arms[5]. By pursuing successfully an honest occupation a man deserved consideration[6]; but it is doubtful whether Langland found this a way to worldly prosperity. He seems rather to imply that the honest worker found his reward—and a very true reward—in God's approbation of his labour.

Like most of his contemporaries, the poet refers very seldom to shipmen, except when he moralises on their strange dependence on the sky and lode-star[7]. He says that the wickedness of his generation prevented them from interpreting the signs of the weather[8]. His only reference to a ship occurs in the description of the Ark[9], which was supposed to resemble a ship made of "schides and bordes," or a "shynglede schip."

COINAGE

The frequent mention in *Piers Plowman* of gold, silver and copper coins suggests that at this time payment was usually made in coin. Gold coins mentioned are the "moton of golde[10]," the florin[11] and the red noble, or gold noble, which bore on one face a cross and on the other the king's head with a crown. When Avarice lent money for "love of the crosse," he was thinking of the cross stamped on the coins[12]. A "pounde of nobles[13]" seems to have been considered a large sum by a poor clerk. Silver coins were more commonly used and the word occurs as a synonym for money[14]. Groats, the commonest silver coins, were also marked with a cross and a king's crown[15]. A groat pur-

1 A v 167; B v 324; C vii 373, cf. 309.　　**2** A v 161, 165; B v 318, 322; C vii 365, 370, 371.　　**3** B p 118; C i 144.　　**4** B xix 229; C xxii 234.　　**5** B iii 322; C iv 480.　　**6** A xi 182; B v 554.
7 B xv 354; C xviii 98, xxii 236.　　**8** B xv 350; C xviii 94.　　**9** A x 160; B ix 131; C xi 222.　　**10** A iii 25; B iii 24; C iv 25.　　**11** A ii 113; B ii 143, iii 156; C iii 157, iv 195.　　**12** B v 244, xv 501, 507; C xviii 200, 207.　　**13** B x 289.　　**14** A ii 112, iii 80; B ii 142, iii 89; C iii 156, iv 116, vi 72.　　**15** A iv 113; B xv 507; C xviii 207.

chased a gallon of best ale[1]. Shillings are only once mentioned[2]. Pence were, naturally, most commonly used; and farthings also are mentioned[3].

The coins were frequently debased by moneylenders, who pared pence[4]. Bad money was brought across the sea from Luxemburg and the "badde peny with a good preynte[5]," made from inferior metal but well-marked, was known as the "Lussheborgh." The old custom of giving a tally, or notching a stick, part of which was retained by the buyer and part by the seller, was still practised[6]; but it was not very popular, since it gave an advantage to the dishonest trader who had "as moche pite of pore men · as pedlere hath of cattes[7]."

Recreations and Public Entertainers

In the fourteenth century there were fewer, or certainly less varied, amusements than now. Dramatic performances rarely took place, and in many cases they were essentially religious functions though comic episodes were introduced. Reading and writing were unfamiliar arts to the greater part of the population. Travelling was only undertaken when necessary, and offered little prospect of recreation. One of the chief amusements of rich and poor alike was story-telling[8]. In the absence of professional talent[9], men entertained each other with the recital of their own deeds[10], or repeated familiar tales such as the adventures of Robin Hood or of Randolf Earl of Chester[11], and at the dinner-table each could take his turn at harping or singing an improvised "fitte[12]."

The frequenters of the tavern sang refrains[13] and played games such as the "New Fair" described fully in *Piers Plowman*[14]. "Clement the cobelere" offered his cloak for sale, and his challenge was accepted by "Hikke the hakeneyman" who cast down his hood and called upon "Bette the bochere" to support him. The intermediaries decided that whoever had the hood

1 A v 138; B v 224; C vii 230.　　**2** C iv 395.　　**3** A p 86, iv 50; B p 212, iii 161, iv 64; C i 161, iv 200, etc.　　**4** B v 242; C vii 241. **5** B xv 342; C xviii 72, 82; Wright, *Political Poems*, p. 140, "John of Bridlington," Prose Commentary.　　**6** A ix 74; B v 429, viii 82; C viii 35, xi 80; A iv 45; B iv 58, v 252; C v 61.　　**7** B v 258.　　**8** B v 383. cf. C vii 435.　　**9** B xiii 58.　　**10** B xiii 304; C vii 50.　　**11** B v 402; C viii 11.　　**12** A i 137; C vii 46.　　**13** A v 190, vii 108; B v 345, vi 117; C vii 396, ix 122.　　**14** A v 170; B v 327; C vii 376.

must be compensated for its inferiority to the cloak, but they could not agree on the terms. "Robyn the ropere," acting as umpire, awarded the cloak to Hikke and arranged that Clement should have the hood and fill his cup at Hikke's expense. Whoever disapproved of this decision was to be fined a gallon of beer. There were, too, outdoor games, such as the "somer-game of souteres[1]." Hunting and hawking, favourite pastimes with the higher classes, were outside Langland's province. He remarks on the need of destroying fox, hare, badger and boar[2]; but speaks of it as the knight's duty[3], and advises prelates and priests to find more suitable employment.

The description of the "Field Full of Folk" suggests that, after business had been transacted, the bargainers feasted and amused themselves[4]; and one of the annual gatherings for merry-making, the cherry fair, is mentioned in *Piers Plowman*[5]. A feature of these fairs and festivals was the presence of wandering minstrels and entertainers. The unflattering implications of the remark that

mynstrales and messagers · mette with Lyere ones,
And with-helde hym half a ȝere · and elleve dayes[6]

are quite in keeping with the view which medieval moralists ordinarily took of contemporary gleemen; but everywhere these wanderers were welcomed by the people. They remained a power in the land and wandered from feast to feast[7]; since no festivity[8] could be held in castle, home or tavern without the minstrel[9], who was sometimes generously paid for his services; few men were "gladdore then the gleo-mon is · of his grete ȝiftes[10]." Ecclesiastics received professional minstrels with favour and helped to support them, though church councils looked upon such patronage with great disfavour. Kings and nobles, anxious to secure their services, included in their households minstrels who enjoyed special privileges. Wherever the royal musicians[11] went they were received with special honour and sometimes placed at the high table in compliment to their master[12]. Minstrels[13] of noble households received similar attentions according to their patron's

1 B v 413.   2 A vii 32; B vi 30; C ix 28.   3 C x 223.   4 A p; B p; C i; Froissart, ii, chap. xxii, Globe Edn, p. 313.   5 B v 161. 6 C iii 237, cf. A ii 203, B ii 227.   7 B x 92.   8 B xiii 442; C viii 102. 9 A xi 39; B x 52; C xii 35.   10 A iii 213, xi 110; B iii 219, x 154; C iv 277, xii 104.   11 B xiii 437; C viii 97.   12 B xiii 444. 13 C x 128.

rank, and were rewarded for their services by gifts of fine clothes, fur-trimmed robes and money[1]. According to Langland, they monopolised alms which should have been given to the needy poor[2].

He comments unfavourably on such hospitality, saying:

> Clerkus and knyʒtes · welcometh kynges mynstrales,
> And for love of here lordes · lithen hem at festes;
> Muche more, me thenketh · riche men auhte
> Have beggers by-fore hem · whiche beth godes mynstrales[3].

The instruments of harpers[4], fiddlers[5] and ribibours[6], or players of the "rebeck," a kind of violin, were used to accompany the voice on festive occasions; but the term minstrelsy covered a wide field in the fourteenth century. Activa-vita mentions some of the popular arts practised by minstrels; when lamenting his own poverty, he says:

> Couthe I lye to do men laughe · thanne lacchen I shulde
> Other mantel or money · amonges lordes mynstralles.
> Ac for I can noither tabre ne trompe · ne telle none gestes,
> Farten, ne fythelen · at festes, ne harpen,
> Jape ne Jogly · ne gentlych pype,
> Ne noyther sailly ne saute · ne synge with the gyterne,
> I have none gode gyftes · of thise grete lordes[7].

Many kinds of entertainers were included in the ranks of minstrels; and some of them probably fully deserved the hard sayings of the moralists. The difficulties and dangers menacing the ordinary minstrel would encourage

> braulyng and bakbytyng · and beryng of fals witnesse[8].

From Langland's account it is difficult to distinguish between the different grades. All ranks of society seem to have taken pleasure in the performances of disours[9], "Japeres and Jogeloures and Jangelers of gestes[10]," "taberes and tomblers" (or drummers and acrobats[11]), the apeward and the gleeman[12], whose dog had been taught to walk upon its hind legs[13].

---

1 B XIII 227, XIV 24; C XVI 202; Froissart, II xxxi, p. 339, Globe Edn; "Glasgerion," verse 4.   **2** B IX 90.   **3** C VIII 97, cf. B XIII 437.   **4** B XIV 24.   **5** B X 92.   **6** A V 165; B V 322; C VII 371.   **7** B XIII 228, cf. C XVI 203.   **8** B XV 232.   **9** A XI 30.   **10** B X 31, XIII 172; C XVI 171.   **11** A II 79.   **12** A VI 119; B V 640; C VIII 284.   **13** A V 197; B V 353; C VII 404. Cf. Skeat, note.

When describing the crowd in the "Field Full of Folk," Langland says that

> somme murthes to make · as mynstrals conneth,
> That wollen neyther swynke ne swete · bote swery grete othes,
> And fynde up foule fantesyes · and foles hem maken,
> And haven witte at wylle · to worche yf they wolde[1].

"Jakke, the jogeloure," idled away his time with "Danyel the dys-playere," "Robyn the rybaudoure" and other undesirable companions[2]. These vagabonds who knew

> namore mynstralcye · ne musyke, men to glade,
> Than Munde the mylnere · of *multa fecit deus*[3]!

shared the popularity of men who

> murthes to make · as mynstralles conneth,
> And geten gold with here glee · synneles[4].

Langland says that, were it not for the minstrels' ribald tales and wanton songs,

> Shulde nevere kyng ne kniȝt · ne chanoun of seynt Poules
> ȝyve hem to her ȝeresȝive · the ȝifte of a grote[5]!

Tales "of bounte of batailes and of treuthe[6]," such as might be told by minstrels who piped before the battle[7], formed only a small part of the entertainer's repertory. The "goliardeys[8]," or glutton of words, as he was called, amused and excited the crowd by ready comments and apt quotations applied from burlesque Latin verse to contemporary events. At their banquets,

> lordes and ladyes · and legates of holicherche[9]

were repaid for their hospitality by flattery. The moralist urged

> Holde with none harlotes · ne here nouȝte her tales,
> And nameliche atte mete · suche men eschue;
> For it ben the develes disoures · I do the to understande[10].

The tellers of ribald stories, or "harlotes[11]," seem to have established themselves as securely "in halle" and in "chambres" as in the tavern[12]. Any indiscreet remark was allowed to pass

---

1 C I 35, cf. below. Cf. B x 43.   2 A vii 65; B vi 72; C ix 71.
3 B x 43.   4 B P 33, cf. A P 33. Cf. C I 35 above.   5 A xi 33;
B x 46.   6 C ix 49, cf. A vii 47, B vi 53.   7 B xx 92; C xxiii 93.
8 B P 139.   9 B xiii 422, cf. C viii 82.   10 B vi 54, cf. A vii 48,
C ix 50.   11 C xii 28.   12 B xiii 434; C vii 369, 435,
viii 94.

and considered entertaining[1] though their hosts were warned that

> flaterers and foles · with here foule wordes
> Leden tho that lithen hem · to Luciferes feste,
> With *turpiloquio*, a lay of sorwe · and Lucifers fithele[2].

Rich men seem to have paid little attention to the moralists' suggestions:

> ich rede ʒow riche · reveles when ʒe maken
> For to solace ʒoure soules · suche mynstrales to have;
> The poure for a fol sage · syttynge at thy table,
> With a lered man, to lere the · what oure lord suffrede
> For to savy thy saule · fram Satan thyn enemye,
> And fithele the, with-oute flateryng · of goode Fryday the geste,
> And a blynde man for a bordiour · other a bedreden womman,
> To crye a largesse by-fore oure lorde · ʒoure goode loos to shewe[3].

BEGGARS

In medieval England, all thoroughfares and public places swarmed with beggars[4]. On Sundays persons who appeared to be blind or maimed sat by the highway[5], and they begged for alms in the churches on Fridays and feast-days[6]. They visited private houses[7], pushed their way roughly through every crowd[8], told boastful tales[9] and fought in the taverns[10]; yet when it suited their purpose their manner changed completely:

> there ar beggeres and bidderes · bedemen as it were,
> Loketh as lambren · and semen lyf-holy,
> Ac it is more to have her mete · with such an esy manere,
> Than for penaunce and parfitnesse · the poverte that such taketh[11].

The beggar was known by his bag, in which he stored money or food[12]. His clothing was only remarkable by reason of its extreme poverty; uncharitable bishops[13], disgusted by his torn clothes, would drive him away while they were willing to give money to buffoons:

> beggeres aboute Midsomer · bredlees thei soupe,
> And ʒit is wynter for hem worse · for wete-shodde thei gange,
> A-fyrst sore and afyngred · and foule yrebuked,
> And a rated of riche men · that reuthe is to here[14].

1 C x 131. 2 B xiii 455; C viii 115. 3 B xiii 442; C viii 102, cf. C x 136. 4 A iii 212; B iii 218; C iv 276. 5 A vii 181. 6 C vi 30. 7 C vi 29. 8 A p 40; B p 40; C i 41. 9 B xiv 213; C xvii 56. 10 B xiii 303; C vii 49, x 98. 11 B xv 199. 12 A xii 71; C x 98, 154; "Robin Hood and the Widow's Sons," verses 11 and 23 (*Ballad Book*, Allingham). 13 B ix 89. 14 B xiv 160, cf. C xvii 13.

In such hard times the beggar was grateful for bread "that was bake for Bayarde[1]" (the horse); but often he did little work, fared sufficiently well and went to bed satisfied, with a bag of scraps[2]:

> Bidders and beggers · faste a-boute eoden,
> Til heor bagges and heore balies · weren bratful I-crommet;
> Feyneden hem for heore foode · fou3ten atte alle;
> In glotonye, God wot · gon heo to bedde,
> And ryseth up with ribaudye · this Roberdes knaves;
> Sleep and sleu3the · suweth hem evere[3].

When he had acquired food and clothing the beggar had achieved his aim. He accepted no responsibility for his fellows[4]; escaping the usual duties of a citizen, such as payment of tithes and serving on juries[5]. This was the only compensation for what was the most miserable existence the poet could imagine[6]; and such hardship encouraged Langland to believe in a future existence[7]:

> Then may beggers, as bestes · after blysse asken,
> That al here lif haven lyved · in langour and defaute.

A few beggars had sunk to this wretched condition through no fault of their own. Amongst these the poet mentions old white-haired men, women, blind and bedridden folk[8], and those with broken limbs, cripples supported with irons, lepers suffering in patience and all who had lost property through fire, flood or the devices of evil men[9]. Rich men were urged to discriminate between these unfortunate creatures and able-bodied vaga-bonds. All men asking alms in God's name were, if possible, to be relieved[10]. If economy were to be practised, the deserving man was to receive alms first[11]. For beggary in general Langland had no respect, though he was always ready to respect the deserving poor whose mendicancy was due to misfortune[12]. Similarly popular opinion denounced mendicancy as a crime for all but religious and disabled persons[13]. But there were many able-bodied men amongst the beggars. A certain number of

---

1 A VII 203; B VI 196, 217; C IX 192, 225.　　2 A VII 130, XII 69; B VI 137; C IX 142.　3 A P 40, cf. B P 40, C I 41.　4 B XV 221; C XVII 349.　5 C XIV 79, 84.　6 C VII 314.　7 C XVI 297, cf. B XIV 116. 8 A VII 131, VIII 83; B VI 138, VII 99; C IX 143, 201, X 175.　9 A VIII 86; B VII 102; C VI 34, X 99, 179.　10 B XI 269.　11 A XI 185. 12 A XI 45; B VII 88, X 58, XII 147, XIII 439; C X 165, VIII 99, XII 42. 13 A VII 202, VIII 68; B VI 216, VII 66; C IX 224, X 61.

idlers pretended they were blind or maimed and stood with men who were really unable to work[1]. Sometimes these impostors, to excite pity, broke their children's bones[2]; and many real deformities resulted from these practices. Amongst such men and women decency and morality were unknown[3]; and the poet likens them to animals. Their rough behaviour was not confined to intercourse amongst themselves—for they offered to molest labourers who did not give them the best of everything[4]. Experience proved that starvation was the best treatment for these vagabonds who scorned both law and the knight's arms. Famine made the poorest gifts acceptable and drove the beggar to work.

Langland several times uses the word "loller" to describe lazy vagabonds[5]. He even gives the name to worthless hermits and justifies himself by referring back to one original meaning of the word:

> Now kyndeliche, by Crist · beth suche callyd "lolleres,"
> As by Englisch of oure eldres · of olde menne techynge.
> He that lolleth is lame · other his leg out of joynte,
> Other meymed in som membre · for to meschief hit souneth.
> And ryght so sothlyche · suche manere eremytes
> Lollen aʒen the byleyve · and lawe of holy churche[6].

Those who do not bear "bagges · ne none botels under clokes' do not lead the life of lollers and such hermits:

> That loken ful louheliche · to lacchen mennes almesse,
> In hope to sitten at even · by the hote coles,
> Unlouke hus legges abrod · other lygge at hus ese,
> Reste hym, and roste hym · and his ryg turne,
> Drynke drue and deepe · and drawe hym thanne to bedde;
> And when hym lyketh and lust · hus leve ys to aryse;
> When he ys rysen, rometh out · and ryght wel aspieth
> Whar he may rathest have a repast · other a rounde of bacon,
> Sulver other sode mete · and som tyme bothe,
> A loof other half a loof · other a lompe of chese;
> And carieth it hom to hus cote · and cast him to lyve
> In ydelnesse and in ese · and by others travayle[7].

Healthy men who led such a life lived in defiance of God's law and the Church[8], says the poet, and Reason, when

---

1 A vii 114, 179; B vi 123, 194; C ix 128, 188.   2 A viii 77; B vii 93; C x 169.   3 A viii 73; B vii 89; C x 166.   4 A vii 140, 193; B vi 154, 207; C ix 149, 211.   5 B xv 207; C vi 2, 4, ix 288, x 159.   6 C x 213.   7 C x 141.   8 C x 103.

questioning him as to how he can afford to live in idleness, reproves him:

an ydel man thow semest,
A spendour that spende mot · other a spille-tyme,
Other beggest thy bylyve · a-boute at menne hacches,
Other faitest up-on Frydays · other feste-dayes in churches,
The whiche is lollarene lyf · that lytel ys preysed[1].

The only excuse for such a life is a broken limb. But with such lollers are contrasted those who

wanteth here witt · men and women bothe,
The whiche aren lunatik lollers · and leperes a-boute,
And mad as the mone sitt · more other lasse.
Thei caren for no cold · ne counteth of no hete,
And arn mevynge after the mone · moneyles thei walke,
With a good wil, witlees · meny wyde contreys,
Ryght as Peter dude and Paul · save that thei preche nat,
Ne myracles maken; · ac meny tymes hem happeth
To prophecien of the puple · pleyinge, as hit were[2].

Such wanderers are said to be holy men and have special privileges:

Barfot and bredles · beggeth thei of no man.
And thauh he mete with the meyre · amyddes the strete,
He reverenceth hym ryght nouht · no rather than another[3].

They deserve entertainment as being the "mynstrales of hevene."

There were other more dangerous mendicants and vagrants, known as "wastours," "brytoneres" (perhaps Breton mercenaries) and "Roberdes knaves," the latter perhaps named after Robin Hood, for "Roberd" or "Robert" was a common name for a thief[4].

Pickpockets and cut-purses frequented the taverns[5]. Certain localities were avoided on dark nights by heavily laden travellers[6], especially if they journeyed alone. No man dared venture unarmed through the pass of Alton, in Hamp-

---

1 C vi 27.　　　　2 C x 106. It is not evident how far Langland would have included Wycliffite Lollards in this category, and how far he uses "loller" in its earlier and looser sense, in which it was applied to all sorts of religious tramps. His attitude towards the "lunatik lollers" is characteristically medieval and still survives in the French "crétin" (=chrétien).　　3 C x 121.　　4 A P 44, V 242, VII 140, 142; B P 44, V 469, VI 154, 156; C I 45, VII 316, IX 149, 152.　　5 A VI 118; B V 639; C VII 370, VIII 283.　　6 C XIV 58.

shire[1]; nor could he spend the night in comfort amongst strangers[2]:

> outlawes in the wode · and under banke lotyeth,
> And may uch man se · and gode merke take,
> Who is bihynde and who bifore · and who ben on hors,
> For he halt hym hardyer on horse · than he that is a fote[3].

"Pykers and theeves" made it necessary to guard the stacks carefully; and on every battlefield there were plunderers or "pyke-herneys[4]."

In many instances theft was accompanied by murder[5], an occurrence probably due to the severity of laws dealing with robbers or "pilours[6]." A thief was sentenced to be hanged in this world and was promised as severe punishments in the next world as a murderer[7]. He might escape justice at the time, but

> he that ys ones a theef · is evere-more in daunger,
> And as the lawe lyketh · to lyve other to deye[8].

1 B xiv 300; C xvii 139.   **2** B v 233; C vii 235.   **3** B xvii 102.
4 B xx 261; C vi 17, xxiii 263.   **5** B xvii 271; C xx 254.
6 B xviii 40; cf. C xxi 39.   **7** B v 236; C vii 238, xviii 138.   **8** C xv 146, cf. B xii 206.

V

WEALTH AND POVERTY OF SOCIETY

THE first part of *Piers Plowman* is a commentary on the tyranny of wealth over Church and State in medieval England. The nation, demoralised by the ravages of the pestilence[1], was passing through a period of unrest and discontent, during which no established authority could cope with the growing desire for luxury. At this time the towns were very prosperous[2]; and the ruling classes, whilst impoverishing themselves and their lands, were enriching the merchants, who were enabled to buy privileges hitherto reserved for the nobility[3]. Sumptuary laws were framed to control expenditure[4]; but both clergy and laity continued to expend money on clothing and on " Maister Johan's " costly food[5]. Langland was grieved by the decline of the nobleman's prestige, but it appears from his account that the commons were amused rather than impressed by the nobles' extravagance[6], and took advantage of their foolish display:

Ich have ylent to lordes and to ladies · that lovede me nevre after.
Ich have mad meny a knyght · bote mercer and draper,
Payede nevere for here prentishode · nauht a payre gloves;
That chaffared with my chyvesaunce · chevede selde after[7].

Thus the merchant boasted of his dishonest dealings, and the nobility were completely in his power, for the ban on usury prevented any self-respecting man from lending money on interest in the ordinary course[8]. Lords and ladies and even the king himself when their estates were exhausted must either replenish their coffers by marriage alliances, or must have recourse to moneylenders[9]. These were either Jews[10], whose

---

1 Wright, *Political Poems*, p. 279, "On the Pestilence."   **2** Wright, *Political Poems*, p. 183, "John of Bridlington."   **3** C VI 72.   **4** Wright, *Political Poems*, p. 399, "On the Deposition of Richard II."   **5** A P 24; B P 24, XIII 278, XIX 282; C I 26, VII 30, XXII 287.   **6** *Richard the Redeless*, III 178.   **7** C VII 249, cf. B V 254.   **8** A II 66; B II 86, III 239, XV 83, XIX 347, 366; C III 91, VII 307, XXII 353; *Liber Albus*, Bk. III, pp. 367, 394; Bk. IV, p. 683; Myrc, *Instructions for Parish Priests*, l. 372.   **9** B V 247; C VII 248; see Women and Marriage.   **10** B V 242; C VII 241.

"tawny tabart[1]" Avarice wore, and who were popularly believed to be condemned to this occupation[2], or "Lombards[3]"
(a term often including all natives of North or Central Italy),
who combined usury with trade.

Both men and women wore materials, splendid in colour and
texture, which were further adorned by clasps of gold, pendant
jewels of silver[4], rings set with rubies, silver girdles, from which
hung purses, and knives with gilded studs on the handle[5]. Fur
was used freely, both as a trimming and as a material in itself.
Certain varieties[6] were reserved for the use of men and women
of high rank, or of men distinguished in their profession[7].
Langland mentions[8] that costly gowns and mantles were made
of miniver[9], squirrel[10] or Calabrian[11] fur.

Of the costly materials in use at the time, the poet mentions
various kinds of silk: Tarse or tartaryne[12], brought from Tartary,
which was used for tunics, sendel[13], from which Church vestments were made, and cammoka[14]. Cipres[15] was a kind of fine
gauze. Scarlet and ray-cloth[16] were materials used only by the
wealthier classes. Fashionable garments were "dagged[17]," or cut
in peaks round the hem, and pointed shoes were worn[18]. Gilt
armour[19] was another extravagance of the last days of chivalry.
Gloves were used by the upper classes[20].

Money was lavished on food; and many cooks and scullions
were employed in preparing the great feasts, at which "wastours"
devoured what poor men earned[21]. Langland mentions many of
the favourite dishes[22]: pottages, baked pheasant, pullets, goose,
wild fowl, spiced meat, tripe, brawn, pork, bacon, venison,

---

1 B v 196.   2 B xviii 106; C xxi 111.   3 C v 194.   4 A vii
257; B vi 272, xv 7.   5 A iii 24, ix 79; B iii 23, viii 87, xv 120, 121;
C iv 24, xi 85; *Richard the Redeless*, iii 140.   6 B xv 7, 215; C xvii
343.   7 A iii 277, vii 256; B iii 294, vi 271, xx 175; C iv 452, ix 292,
xxiii 176.   8 B xiii 227; C xvi 202; Froissart, Globe Edn, i cxxii,
p. 95; ii cxcviii, p. 432.   9 B xx 137; C xxiii 138.   10 B xv 215;
C xvii 343.   11 A vii 257; B vi 272; C ix 293.   12 B xv 163, 214, 224.
13 A vii 19; B vi 11; C ix 10.   14 C xvii 299.   15 B xv 224.
16 A iii 277; B xv 163; C xvii 299; "Alison Gross," verse 3; "A Lytell Geste
of Robyn Hode," iv 26, Allingham, *Ballad Book*.   17 B xx 142;
C xxiii 143.   18 B xx 218; C xxiii 219; Wright, *Political Poems*, "On
the Times 1388."   19 B xv 215; C xvii 343.   20 B v 256; C vii 251,
xiv 48.   21 A P 22, vii 272; B P 22, vi 287, x 81; C i 24, ix 309,
xii 66.   22 A P 104, 105, vii 267, 268, 272; B P 225, 226, v 93, 293,
vi 282, 283, 287, x 363, xiii 41, 61, 62, 63, 91, xv 455, xix 283; C i 226,
227, vii 341, ix 304, 305, 309, x 254, xvi 47, 65, 66, 67, 100, xxii 288.

colopys, or slices of meat[1], mortreus, or pounded meat, with milk, sauce, eggs fried in grease, blammanger, hot pies and puddings, Essex cheese. Wastel bread, or white bread, was a luxury, wine was drunk by all who could afford it and there was pomade, a kind of cyder, a precious drink[2]. Apples, pears and plums, and cherries were the commonest kinds of fruit[3].

Though some of the dishes mentioned were delicacies, the greater part of the population seem to have had sufficient plain and wholesome food. Even the labourers, whenever possible, as at harvest time, lived extravagantly on the best food obtainable[4].

Amongst luxuries of the age the poet mentions cups and goblets of silver and pure gold[5]. High houses were regarded as a good investment for money[6]; but the use of private sitting-rooms was still unusual[7]. Pen and parchment were the usual writing materials in use[8].

But while this extravagance was one of the features of the age and labourers required higher wages, the hard-working artisans and their families seem to have suffered, and from Langland's account, the

> poure folke in cotes,
> Charged with children · and chef lordes rente[9],

led a miserable existence after the pestilence. The housewife attempted to add to the craftsman's earnings, and struggled to eke out meal and milk for her children. To such poor folk gifts of bread and penny-ale were welcome as a king's ransom; and cold meat or fish afforded a banquet. Even a meal of mussels or cockles was acceptable on fast-days. Bacon seems to have been a common dish[10]; but only by forgoing necessities could the poor man obtain ale which other men drank by the gallon and gill, and wine was rarely tasted[11]:

> For his rentes ne wol nauȝte reche · no riche metes to bugge;
> And thouȝ his glotonye be to gode ale · he goth to cold beddynge,
> And his heved un-heled · un-esiliche i-wrye;
> For whan he streyneth hym to streche · the strawe is his schetes[12].

1 But see *N.E.D.* which shows that the word was often used also for eggs and bacon. 2 C xxi 412. 3 A vii 281; B vi 295, 296, xvi 69; C ix 311, 318, xiii 221, xix 61. 4 A vii 295; B vi 309; C ix 331. 5 A iii 23; B iii 22; C iv 23. 6 A iii 76; B iii 85; C iv 84, xii 69. 7 B x 94. 8 B ix 38. 9 C x 72; Froissart, Globe Edition, i ccclxxxi, pp. 250, 251; Wright, *Political Poems*, p. 272, "On the Times 1388." 10 B v 194; C vii 201. 11 A v 191; B v 346, xiv 250; C vii 397, xvii 92. 12 B xiv 230, cf. C xvii 73.

Retailers of food made matters all the more difficult for the poor man by charging excessive prices to those "that percel-mel buggen[1]."

The clothing of the "Seven Deadly Sins" gives some idea of the garments worn by poor people at this time. One was dressed in kirtle and "courtepy[2]," or cloak, made of a coarse material known as "caurimaury"; he carried a knife by his side. Sir Hervy wore a torn "tabart[3]" (or sleeveless jacket) of "welch" (which was possibly Welsh flannel) of "twelve winters' age," filthy beyond description and threadbare, since its owner symbolised "Covetousness." He wore a hood on his head. Another person possessed no other garment than the one which he wore[4]. Russet and grey were the serviceable colours usually worn by poor persons[5]. The same extreme poverty marked the furniture of the poor man's "cote[6]." Straw with a blanket usually formed his bed[7]; but sometimes there was no blanket[8]. There were no "almaries" (or cupboards), or iron-bound coffers[9]; all the family treasures were contained in baskets. There were few conveniences for the work at which the father toiled day and night:

glowynge gledes · gladeth nat these workemen
That worchen and waken · in wynteres nyghtes,
As doth a kyx other a candele · that cauht hath fuyr, and blaseth[10].

The poet's insistence on the necessity of possessing wealth, in his later revisions, may perhaps show how the gulf between rich and poor had widened in the years following the pestilence. Langland continually discusses the question of riches and poverty; and he seems to have found difficulty in reconciling the popular view of poverty as a virtue with his own experiences of a struggle for existence[11]. Though he frequently states that "unkynde rychesse[12]" brings additional responsibilities and encourages pride[13], he could not forget the fair dwellings, good

1 A III 72; B III 81; C IV 81.   2 A V 62; B V 79, cf. B VI 191, C IX 185.
3 A V III, cf. B V 196, C VII 203.   4 B XIV 1.   5 A IX 1; B VIII 1,
XV 162, 214; C XI 1, XVII 298, 342.   6 B XII 147; C VI 2, X 72, XV 90
7 B XIV 233; C XVII 76.   8 C X 254.   9 B XIV 245; C XVII 87.
10 C XX 183, cf. B XVII 217.   11 B XIV 108, 212, 279, XIX 63, XX 35;
C XVI 289, XVII 55, 121, XXII 67, XXIII 35.   12 C XV 19.   13 A XI
225; B X 83, 336, XII 46, 245, XIV 132, 203, 215; C XII 68, XIII 205, XVII 1
46, 58.

food and clothing, which were the rich man's portion[1] in this world:

> Ac pore peple, thi prisoneres · lorde, in the put of myschief,
> Conforte tho creatures · that moche care suffren
> Thorw derth, thorw drouth · alle her dayes here,
> Wo in wynter tymes · for wantyng of clothes,
> And in somer tyme selde · soupen to the fulle[2].

He suggests that a higher standard of conduct is required of the wealthy; since, otherwise, they would never experience any discomfort than death. But he also asserts that

> the moneye of this molde · that men so faste kepeth,

might, if put to good use, bring a blessing to its possessor. Though the greatest reward belongs to him who voluntarily seeks poverty, the rich man might help his fellows by assisting the deserving poor.

1 B xiv 157; C xiii 246, xvii 12.   2 B xiv 174.

VI

THE LAYMAN'S RELIGION

LANGLAND summarises, quite briefly, the duties imposed on every member of society by the medieval Church, the "god daughter" of the "great God" and the only means of salvation[1]:

> holy churche hoteth · alle manere puple
> Under obedience to bee · and buxum to the lawe.
> Furst, religious, of religion · here ruele to holde,
> And under obedience to be · by dayes and by nyghtes;
> Lewede men to laborie; · and lordes to honte
> In frythes and in forestes · for fox and other bestes
> That in wilde wodes ben · and in wast places,
> As wolves that wyryeth men · wommen and children;
> And up-on Sonedayes to cesse · godes servyce to huyre,
> Bothe matyns and messe · and, after mete, in churches
> To huyre here evesong · every man ouhte.
> Thus it by-longeth for lorde · for lered, and lewede,
> Eche halyday to huyre · hollyche the service,
> Vigiles and fastyngdayes · forthere-more to knowe,
> And fulfille tho fastynges · bote infirmite hit made,
> Poverte other othere penaunces · as pilgrymages and travayles.
> Under this obedience · arn we echone;
> Who-so brekyth this, be wel war · bot yf he repente,
> Amende hym and mercy aske · and meekliche hym shryve,
> Ich drede me, and he deye · hit worth for dedlich synne
> A-counted by-fore Crist · bote conscience excuse hym[2].

Such was the life recommended by Langland as befitting the members of a Church which he defined as

> Charite...
> Lyf, and Love, and Leaute · in o by-leyve and lawe,
> A love-knotte of leaute · and of leel by-leyve,
> Alle kynne cristene · clevynge on o wyl,
> With-oute gyle and gabbynge · gyve and selle and lene[3].

But he urges the necessity of regarding these observances as inefficacious without good deeds and genuine belief[4].

1 A I 73; B I 75, II 29; C I 138, II 72, III 33.   2 C X 219 ff.
3 C XVIII 125.   4 B X 230; C XII 142.

Baptism is mentioned many times; it was, for the layman, one of the most important of the sacraments[1]:

For a baptized man may · as maistres telleth,
Thorugh contricioun come · to the heigh hevene;
. . . .
Ac a barne with-oute bapteme · may nou3t so be saved[2].

Indeed, speaking of the child, Langland says:

Til it be crystened in Crystes name · and confermed of the bisshop,
It is hethene as to heveneward · and helpelees to the soule[3].

The god-parents were threatened with purgatory[4] if they failed to discharge their duties, but less stress is laid on the importance of confirmation[5]. So important was the first sacrament, that in cases of emergency it might be performed by any of the laity; even

an uncristene... · may cristene an hethene[6].

In criticism of severe remarks made by clerks in their sermons that

noyther Sarasenes ne Jewes,
Ne no creature of Cristes lyknesse · with-outen Crystendome worth
    saved[7],

Langland frequently mentions the salvation of Trajan, "an uncristene creature" though a "trewe knyght[8]":

he is saf, seith the bok · and his soule in hevene[9].

Then he expounds the doctrine that

Ther is follyng of font · and follyng in blod-shedynge,
And thorw fuyr is follyng · and al is ferm by-leyve[10];

continuing to assert his belief that moral virtue, unsupported by ritual, is worthy of recognition:

Ac treuthe, that trespassede nevere · ne transversede a3ens the lawe,
Bote lyvede as his lawe tauhte · and leyveth ther be no bettere,
And yf ther were, he wolde · and in suche a wil deyeth—
Wolde nevere trewe god · bote trewe treuthe were a-lowed[11].

The knowledge that the Penitent Thief and Mary Magdalene are in paradise emboldens him to believe that virtuous pagans will

1 A xii 15; B xi 113, xiv 183, xvii 94, xviii 374, xix 39; C xiii 52, xx 86, xxi 421, xxii 39.   2 B xi 80.   3 B xv 449.   4 B ix 74. 5 B xv 545; C xviii 268.   6 A xi 232, cf. B x 350.   7 B xii 276, cf. C xv 201.   8 B xi 136, xii 210; C xiii 75, xv 150.   9 C xv 206, cf. B xii 280.   10 C xv 207, cf. B xii 282.   11 C xv 209, cf. B xii 284.

be saved[1]. He questions whether it is reasonable to believe of David and Paul that

> now ben thise as sovereynes · wyth seyntes in hevene,
> Tho that wrou3te wikkedlokest · in worlde tho thei were.
> And tho that wisely wordeden · and wryten many bokes
> Of witte and of wisdome · with dampned soules wonye[2].

Thus he argues that Aristotle, Socrates and Solomon must be saved by a just God:

> god is so good, ich hope · sitthe he gaf hem wittes
> To wissen ous weyes ther-with · that wenen to be saved,
> And the bettere for here bookes— · to bidden we been holde
> That god for hus grace · gyve here saules reste[3].

But the sacrament of which Langland gives the fullest account is that of Confession, which, with penance, he recommends on every possible occasion[4]:

> who so loveth Joye,
> To penaunce and to poverte · he moste putten hym-selven,
> And moche wo in this worlde · willen and suffren[5].

The prayers and lifelong penance of saints were the most acceptable offering that could be made[6]:

> Preyers of a parfyt man · and penaunce discret
> Ys the leveste labour · that oure lord pleseth[7].

The mediation of the Saints had won penance as a concession to sinners[8]; and by it a man might escape from "derkenesse and drede and the devel[9]." Langland's "Palace of Truth[10]" was built by and entered through acts of penance which he regarded as the sinner's last chance[11].

Common sense seems to have suggested most of the penances recommended in *Piers Plowman*. He says that he himself went "wolleward and wete-shoed[12]," and he recommends a hair-shirt as a remedy against pride[13]. The Lady fast on Saturday and the Friday fast were for the intemperate, and regular attendance at church service was required of the idler[14]. The covetous sinner

---

1 B x 414; C xii 254. 2 B x 426, cf. C xii 269. 3 C xv 195, cf. B xii 270. 4 A v; B v, xii 176, xiv 82, xix 328, xx 212; C vii, viii, xv 115, xvii 26, xxii 333, xxiii 213. 5 B xix 62, cf. C xxii 66. 6 A viii 104; B vii 119. 7 C vi 84. 8 C iv 100. 9 B xv 543, xvi 85; C xviii 266, xix 117. 10 A vi 88; B v 607; C viii 247. 11 A viii 163; B vii 177, xiii 412, xvi 38, xvii 95, xix 374; C viii 72, x 236, 328, xix 41, xxii 378. 12 B xviii 1, cf. C xxi 1. 13 A v 48; B v 66; C vii 6. 14 A v 57, 219, 232; B v 74, 389, 458; C vii 173, 439, viii 65; Myrc, *Instructions for Parish Priests*, lines 1667 to 1784.

was advised to restore illegal profits[1] to his victims, and those who could give money were ordered to

> amende *mesondieux*... · and myseyse folke helpe,
> And wikked wayes · wiȝtlich hem amende;
> And do bote to brugges · that to-broke were,
> Marien maydenes · or maken hem nonnes;
> Pore peple and prisounes · fynden hem here fode,
> And sette scoleres to scole · or to somme other craftes;
> Releve religioun · and renten hem bettere[2].

Suffering in patience was also recommended as a penance[3]. In his advice to

> Kytte my wyf and Kalote · my doughter

he mentions the Good Friday penance known as creeping to the cross:

> Ariseth and reverenceth · goddes resurrexioun,
> And crepeth to the crosse on knees · and kisseth it for a Juwel[4]!

Pilgrimage was one of the usual penances; this was regarded by the poet with mistrust in practice, though he approved the original motives[5]. At one time it had been a very severe punishment, and Langland has no doubt that the true-hearted pilgrim[6] earns by his present sufferings much relief from future purgatory. But not all pilgrims, by any means, were so sincere, and the popularity of pilgrimage as a penance had resulted in provision being made as far as possible for the pilgrim's comfort. The pilgrim or palmer, with bag, bowl and burdon, or staff, with its twist of cloth, became a familiar figure[7]; and by the time that his patience and poverty had become proverbial, all pilgrims enjoyed, as a right, privileges which had been won by their predecessors[8]. In certain places, rendered specially sacred by the presence of some conspicuous "corseint" or holy relic[9], accommodation was provided for pilgrims; and they usually travelled for safety and comfort in large parties, either riding or walking[10]. The shrines of St James, St Thomas, those at Rome and Walsingham, the crosses of Bromholm, Lucca and Chester are all men-

---

1 B v 232; C vii 234. 2 B vii 26, cf. A viii 28, C x 30. 3 B xiv 10; Pecock, *Repressor*, Part ii, pp. 207, 269. 4 B xviii 427; C xxi 474. 5 A v 260, vii 77; B v 517, vi 86, xix 373, xx 378; C viii 155, ix 93, xxii 377, xxiii 380. 6 C x 180. 7 A vi 10, vii 53; B v 526, vi 59; C viii 164, ix 56. 8 B xi 234, xiii 29; C xiii 130, xvi 34. 9 A vi 23; B v 539; C viii 177; *Priory of Coldingham*, Surtees Society, 1841, i 231, Letter ccxxxiv. 10 A p 46; B p 46; C i 47.

tioned by Langland[1], and he refers to Rocamadour, Bethlehem, Babylon, India and Damascus, as being visited on account of the great events which had been enacted there. A palmer who had visited many of these places and carried away tokens is described thus:

> He bar a bordon ybounde · with a brod lyste,
> In a weythwynde wyse · ywrythe al aboute;
> A bolle and a bagge · he bar by hus syde,
> And an hondred hanypeles · on hus hatte seten,
> Signes of Syse · and shilles of Galys,
> And meny crouche on hus cloke · and keyes of Rome,
> And the fernycle by-fore · for men sholde knowe,
> And se by hus sygnes · wham he souht hadde[2].

As might be expected, the true object of the pilgrimage was sometimes lost sight of, especially when the pilgrim related his adventures and produced his treasures[3]. He might make any additions he chose to his story, since those who stayed at home could not contradict him. Even the palmer described above was not to be accepted as a trustworthy guide to Truth. Langland, forestalling a suggestion of the heretics, suggests that the time would be spent better in caring for sick men in prisons and hovels[4]. He especially distrusted "Rome-renners."

The sinner sometimes tried to evade such penances and ensure safety for his soul by acquiring papal indulgences; which were naturally vouched by papal bulls. Our author seems to hint that the mere act of buying a papal bull was often supposed to confer absolution on the purchaser[5], but we must remember that "purchase" meant "procure." Though Langland would not denounce such papal bulls, he says that such grants, together with triennials, provincials' letters or bishops' letters, were less valuable than a well-spent life[6]. But he openly attacked the various substitutions for corporal penance, recommended by the friars[7], who enriched themselves by the proceeds. The friar acting

---

1 A P 47, 51, IV 109 ff., V 40, 144, 240, VI 1, 48, VII 93; B P 47, 54, IV 126 ff., V 57, 230, 467, 566, VI 102, XII 37; C I 48, 52, V 122 ff., VI 198, VIII 201, IX 109.   2 C VIII 162, cf. A VI 8, B V 524.   3 A P 49; B P 49; C I 50; Foxe, *Acts and Monuments*, vol. III, p. 268, "Examination of Wm Thorpe 1409," 3rd Point; Chaucer, *Hous of Fame*, Book III, line 2122. 4 A IV 111, V 40; B IV 128, V 57, XV 177; C V 122, 125, VI 198, XVII 321; Foxe, *Acts*, V 34, "John Hewes, draper, A.D. 1531."   5 A VIII 173; B VII 186; C X 337.   6 A VIII 156; B VII 169, XVII 252; C X 319, XX 218. 7 See The Friars.

as confessor lost no opportunity of benefiting his Order; he suggested:

> We have a wyndow a worchyng · wol stonden ous ful hye;
> Wolde ȝe glase the gable · and grave ther ȝoure name,
> In masse and in matyns · for Mede we shulleth synge
> Solenliche and sothlich · as for a sustre of oure ordre[1].

From a spiritual point of view Langland also condemned the mercenary marriages which seem to have been common in these years following the pestilence[2]. He disapproved of divorce and placed before married men and women a high ideal of purity and obedience to the law[3]. But the principles of monastic teaching were deeply rooted; so that Langland, while paying his tribute to the diligence and thrift of married folk[4], reserves his loudest praise for those who remained faithful to the ascetic ideal. Matrimony hangs lowest on the Tree of Life, beneath celibacy and widowhood[5].

The sacrament of extreme unction is passed over without mention; though Langland argues the need of confession from the plight of those who carried to their deathbed the sins of a lifetime without securing the Almighty's promise of redemption[6]:

> ich shal sende ȝow my-selve · seynt Michel myn angel,
> That no devel shal ȝow dere · ne despeir in ȝoure deyinge,
> And sende ȝoure soules · ther ich my-self dwelle,
> And there a-byde body and soule · in blisse for evere[7].

The dying man might attempt to ensure salvation for his soul by his will, in which he might insert the clause:

> The chirche schal have my careyne · and kepe mi bones;

with the words:

> He schal have my soule · that best hath deservet,
> And defende hit from the fend[8].

But the laxity of executors in carrying out the wishes of the dead was notorious, and even the clergy could not be trusted to perform their duties.

Langland's attitude to oaths shows that he was no Lollard. Even Piers Plowman does not hesitate to swear "By seynt Peter

---

1 C IV 51, cf. A III 49, B III 48.   2 A X 191; B IX 171; C XI 279. 3 A X 196; B IX 184, XII 35, XX 137; C XI 291, XXIII 138.   4 A X 127; B IX 107; C XI 202; Wyclif, ed. Arnold, III 190, "Of Weddid Men and Wifis and of here Children also."   5 B XII 39, XVI 68; C XIX 86. 6 B XVII 306; C XX 288.   7 C X 37, cf. A VIII 36, B VII 33.   8 A VII 80, cf. B VI 89, C IX 96.

of Rome,' "'By seynt Poule," or even "bi Crist[1]." There are fairly frequent instances of such oaths as "bi Crist" or "bi Marie of heuene" passing unreproved[2]. Such typical medieval oaths as that of the "beau frere," named Book, "a bold man of speche[3]," who swears "by Godes body," were usually considered offensive, and idle swearing was condemned[4]. Perjury was, of course, a grave offence. The merchants, however, endangered their future happiness by swearing

bi heore soule · —"so god hem moste helpe! "—
A3eyn heore clene concience · heore catel to sulle[5].

Glutton, when confessing his past misdeeds, mentioned this sin first of all:

"I, Glotoun," quod the gome · "gylti me 3elde,
That I have trespassed with my tonge · I can nou3te telle how ofte,
Sworen 'goddes soule' · and 'so god me help and halidom,'
There no nede ne was · nyne hundreth tymes[6]."

It was impossible for laymen to attend all church services; for this reason they were warned specially against neglecting the Sunday services or failing to hallow holy days such as feasts and vigils[7]. Piers Plowman included in his directions to Truth:

hold wel thyn halyday · heye tyl even[8].

He approves of the Church's attitude in regarding the Sabbath as a day of rest and includes feast days and vigils amongst holy days. However important the lady's sewing might be, it was to be put aside

3if hit beo haly day · or elles holy even[9].

Thus

Hewes in the halyday · after hete wayten,
They care no3t thauh it be cold · knaves, when thei worchen[10].

The church services were varied on the great festival days, such as Corpus Christi day, by special chants and reading[11]. On Palm Sunday there was the boys' singing of "gloria laus" and the older folk sang "osanna" to the organ accompaniment[12]. When Easter day dawned "men rang to the resurreccioun[13]," as a warning

1 A vii 3, 262, 272; B vi 3, 25, cf. A vii 27; B vi 277, 287; C ix 1, 298, 309.　　2 A vii 23, xi 228; B vi 22, x 345, xi 27; C ix 19, xii 189.　　3 C xxi 241, cf. B xviii 230.　　4 B xx 224; C xxiii 225. 5 A viii 23, cf. B vii 21, C x 25.　　6 B v 374, cf. C vii 425.　　7 B xiii 384; C vii 272.　　8 C viii 226, cf. A vi 69, B v 588.　　9 A vii 12. 10 C ii 124.　　11 B xv 381; C xviii 120.　　12 B xviii 8; C xxi 6. 13 C xxi 472, cf. B xviii 425.

that laymen should creep to the cross and do reverence to it. But, in spite of restrictions and suggestions as to the hallowing of the holy days, the Church's high ideal seems to have been seldom realised. Many, besides the beggars[1], who were not required to conform to this custom, were lax in their observance of holy days. Tavern-keepers[2] worked, since they must make special provision for fast days. Merchants[3], too, continued to work. Those who abstained from working spent their leisure in self-indulgence. It was on Friday that Glutton turned aside from shrift to enter Beton's tavern[4]. Sloth confessed:

> Ich am ocupied eche day · haly day and other,
> With ydel tales atte nale · and other-whyle in churches;
> Godes pyne and hus passion · is pure selde in my thouhte[5].

Lechour did not observe the Saturday fast and, from his confession, fast days and high festival evenings seem sometimes to have been distinguished by immorality rather than piety[6].

Langland has little to say of the heathen beyond advising Christians to help them to be baptised[7]; but he seems to have shared the interest most medieval churchmen took in Jews and Saracens, whose form of worship in many respects resembled Christianity[8]. He draws attention to the fact that many Christian virtues were practised by Jews and Saracens[9]; but he says their religious zeal could not be acceptable to God since it was founded on a false belief[10]. He urges his fellow-Christians to preach the true belief to them[11], in preparation for their final conversion in an age of miracles[12].

Various strange doctrines current at this time could not be ignored, but Langland always tries to direct the layman's attention from these to good deeds[13]:

> Theologie hath teened me · ten score tymes,
> The more ich muse ther-on · the mystiloker hit semeth,
> And the deppere ich devyne · the derker me thynketh hit.
> Hit is no science sothliche · bote a sothfast by-leyve;
> Ac for hit lereth men to lovye · ich by-leyve ther-on the bettere[14].

1 C xiv 81.   2 B v 381; C vii 434.   3 A viii 22; B vii 20 ; C x 24.   4 C vii 352.   5 C viii 18, cf. B v 409.   6 A v 57; B v 74, xiii 349; C vii 173, 182.   7 B x 365, xv 450.   8 B xviii 92, xix 34; C xxi 96, xxii 34.   9 B ix 81; C xviii 132, 156.   10 B xviii 257; C xxi 270.   11 B xv 386, 404, 492, 596; C xviii 123, 183, 252, 317. 12 B iii 325, xiii 209; C iv 483.   13 A i 160; B i 184; C ii 183, xv 13. 14 C xii 129, cf. A xi 136, B x 180.

The friars and preachers are accused of fostering a spirit of enquiry:

Freres and fele other maistres · that to the lewed men prechen,
ȝe moeven materes inmesurables · to tellen of the trinite,
That ofte tymes the lewed peple · of hir bileve douten.
Bettere byleve were mony · doctoures such techyng,
And tellen men of the ten comaundementz · and touchen the sevene synnes,
And of the braunches that burgeouneth of hem · and bryngeth men to helle,
And how that folke in folyes · myspenden her fyve wittes,
As wel freres as other folke · folilich spenen
In housyng, in haterynge · and in-to hiegh clergye shewynge,
More for pompe than for pure charite[1].

Even at the dinner-table the conversation turned on discussion of the fall of man and other mysteries[2] which, Langland says, should not be discussed, since

hit suffise for oure savacion · sothfast by-leyve[3].

Though his own freedom of thought was remarkable, he was naturally doubtful lest the general discussion of spiritual matters should lead men to question the divine wisdom[4]. Clerks (or as in the latter version, bishops and books) were sufficient for the layman's instruction in such matters as he might wish to learn[5]. Discussion of heresies was forbidden both to clerks and laymen on the grounds that it prepared the way for profanity[6]. There is one slight and casual reference[7] to the chance of being burnt for heresy—a punishment which was decreed in Canon Law and tacitly accepted by the English, as well as by all other states, long before the passing of the Statute "De Hæretico Comburendo." Langland attributes many of the disorders of the age to the decay of faith[8], which was the most desirable virtue for the layman:

so is pruyde en-hansed
In religion and al the reame · among ryche and poure,
That preyeres han no power · these pestilences to lette.
For god is def now a dayes · and deyneth nouht ous to huyre,
And good men for oure gultes · he al to-grynt to dethe[9].

---

1 B xv 68, cf. C xvii 230.   2 A xi 60 ff.; B x 101 ff.   3 C xviii 119, cf. B xv 380.   4 A xi 293; B x 452; C xii 286.   5 B xv 571; C xviii 296.   6 A xi 38; B x 51, xvii 136; C xii 35, xx 110.   7 B xv 81. 8 B xiv 81, xvi 176, xvii 20; C xix 186, xx 22.   9 C xii 58 ff., cf. B x 75 ff.

He gives a long description[1] of the abnormal conditions of the
age in which faith was decreasing:

> Neither the see ne the sande · ne the seed 3eldeth
> As thei woned were; · in wham is defaute?
> Nat in god that he nys good · and the grounde bothe;
> And the see and the seed · the sonne and the mone
> Don her dever day and ny3t · and yf we duden also,
> Ther sholde be plente and pees · perpetuel for evere.

The question of man's responsibility was tackled several times
by Langland, who seems to have been much perplexed by the
problem of destiny and free-will; for he found it hard to recon-
cile the Church's records with either of the theories set forth[2].
He could not definitely set aside the thought that

> how I werche in this world · wrong other ellis,
> I was markid, withoute mercy · and myn name entrid
> In the legende of lif · longe er I were;
> Or ellis undir-writen for wykkid · as witnessith the gospel[3].

But on the whole he seems to have inclined to a more hopeful
view[4]: the master-friar of the Minorites says:

> Ever is thi soule saaf · bote 3if thi-self wolle.
> Folewe thi flessches wil · and the fendes aftur,
> And do dedlich sunne · and drenche thi-selven,
> God wol soffre the dye so · for thi-self hast the maistrie[5].

This was the greatest argument in favour of observing the
Church's precepts[6]:

> uche wi3t in this world · that hath wys understondinge,
> Is cheef sovereyn of him-self · his soule for to 3eme,
> And chevesschen him from charge · whon he childhode passeth,
> Save him-self from sunne · for so him bi-hoveth;
> For worche he wel other wrong · the wit is his oune[7].

Such definite teaching[8] as to the possibility of salvation opposed
the growth of fatalism which too often led to wanhope, or
despair:

> In which flode the fende · fondeth a man hardest[9].

Langland, like most of his contemporaries, held a creed which
was deeply tinged with dualism; to him everything was big with
supernatural importance, whether of God or of the devil. Plain

---

1 C xviii 85, cf. B xv 347.   2 A xi 271; B x 414, xv 258; C xii 254.
3 A xi 252, cf. B x 375, C xii 205.   4 C viii 145.   5 A ix 44, cf.
B viii 49, C xi 51.   6 B xvi 27; C xix 31.   7 A x 71.
8 B xiii 428; C viii 88.   9 B xii 180; C xv 119.

warnings were read in the skies[1], and natural portents were interpreted as tokens of divine displeasure, by men whose recollections of the terror of the pestilence were keen. It was murmured:

> that thuse pestilences
> Was for pure synne · to punyshe the puple;
> And the south-west wynd · on Saterday at eve
> Was pertelich for prude · and for no poynt elles.
> Piries and plomtrees · were poffed to the erthe
> In ensample to syggen ous · we sholde do the betere;
> Beches and brode okes · weren blowe to the grounde,
> And turned upward here tayl · in tokenynge of drede
> That dedlich synne er domys day · shal for-do ous alle[2].

There was little satisfaction to be obtained from this doctrine, and men with a sense of justice complained that the innocent were punished with the guilty[3]. It aroused discontent amongst those whose fortune depended on the elements. One who depended for his livelihood on the harvest confesses:

> Bote ich hadde wedir at my wil · ich wited god the cause[4].

The willingness of the Church to recognise the devil's interference in worldly affairs, and to speak of the triumph of evil over good, in the reign of antichrist, increased superstition[5]. The fallen angels were said to dwell

> Summe in the eir, and summe in the eorthe · and summe in helle deope[6],

and spirits were supposed to aid those who proffered allegiance to the devil, and even to accompany them wherever they went on the earth[7]. The constant reference[8] to witchcraft caused many of the population to have recourse at one time or other to sorcerers, the priests of devil-worship[9]. Charms were popular; precious stones[10] were supposed to possess powers of protecting their wearers. Mention of a magic mirror[11] suggests that Eastern stories of the supernatural were becoming well known. The

---

1 B III 325, VI 327, XV 352; C IV 483, IX 348, XVIII 96; Wright, *Political Poems*, I, p. 250, "On the Earthquake of 1382." 2 C VI 115, cf. A V 13, B V 13. 3 C IV 103. 4 C VII 113. 5 B XIX 214, XX 52; C XXII 219, XXIII 53; "Complaint of the Ploughman," Part II 3, p. 318, III 15, p. 328. 6 A I 114, cf. B I 123; *The Mirror of Perfection*, sect. IX, chap. xcviii. 7 B XVIII 46, 69, 297; C XXI 46, 72, 336; Walsingham, *Historia Anglicana*, I, p. 290, A.D. 1360. 8 B XVI 120; C XIX 150; Froissart, Globe Edition, II xxxvii, p. 354. 9 B XIII 168, 338; C VII 81, 191; Froissart, Globe Edition, II ccvi, p. 440. 10 B II 14. 11 B XI 8; C XII 170.

miraculous powers of saints were said to linger in their personal possessions, and such relics as portions of the Cross were regarded as affording protection against all kinds of evil[1]. The constant reference to "a wel perilous place that purgatorie hette" encouraged interest in the after life[2]. Men were eager to communicate with the unseen world, and availed themselves of dreams, visions, necromancy and the sister sciences[3]. Langland confesses that he meditated many times on his vision[4]; but he placed little value on the interpretation of dreams:

I have no savoure in songewarie · for I se it ofte faille[5].

Laymen were instructed in the mysteries of religion by sermons, miracle or morality plays and didactic writings. Reminiscences of these occur in *Piers Plowman*, since Langland probably derived much of his material from them. Two themes, common in didactic literature, can be traced throughout the poem[6]; life as a pilgrimage, and the struggle between good and evil forces. Every action of life becomes symbolical; the pilgrim on his way to the Palace of Truth is surrounded by the precepts of his religion in the form of mountains and streams[7]. The prioress unconsciously eats "joutes of jangles[8]" prepared by Wrath, and the master-friar refuses dishes symbolising the Christian doctrines[9]. The Church sacraments alone can cleanse Haukyn's coat[10]. The human body is the Castle of Kind[11]; and the Tree of Charity and Tree of Life are mentioned[12].

Langland, like other moralists, draws parallels to explain the Christian mysteries. To him the Christian's attempts to cleanse his soul suggest the laundress's work among the soiled clothes[13]. There is, too, a minute comparison between the Trinity and a hand[14] or a torch[15]. These subtleties, when carried to excess, are bewildering; but probably contemporary readers were impressed by the writer's skill[16].

---

1 B XVIII 430; C XXI 478; *Life of St Francis*, chap. VII, para. 11; chap. XII, para. 11.   **2** A II 71, VII 44, XI 248; B II 103, VI 45, X 370, XI 128, XVIII 390; C III 108, XIII 67, XIX 15.   **3** A P 6; B P 6; Robert of Brunne, *Handlyng Synne*, ed. Furnivall, lines 339 to 500.   **4** A VIII 132; B VII 143; C X 297.   **5** B VII 148, cf. C X 301.   **6** *Piers Plowman*, D. L. Owen, pp. 63, 76.   **7** A VI 50; B V 568; C VIII 204.   **8** B V 158; C VII 133.   **9** B XIII 39; C XVI 45.   **10** B XIV 16.   **11** A X 2; B IX 2; C XI 128.   **12** B XVI 4; C XIX 9.   **13** B XV 181; C XVII 328. **14** B XVII 137; C XX 110.   **15** B XVII 203; C XX 168.   **16** C IV 292.

Similarly, by classification, theology was simplified for the layman. He was taught to recognise five senses[1], seven deadly sins with their branches[2], and four cardinal virtues[3]. "Clergy" had seven sons, elsewhere mentioned as the seven arts and the brothers of Scripture[4].

The religious drama coloured the imaginations of laymen as it did that of Langland; some of the finest passages in *Piers Plowman* appear to have been suggested by plays. The opening scene, as Skeat suggests, recalls the arrangements by which the various abodes of God, devil and man were represented:

> I was in a wildernesse · wuste I never where,
> And as I beo-heold in-to the est · an-hei3 to the sonne,
> I sauh a tour on a toft · tri3ely i-maket;
> A deop dale bi-neothe · a dungun ther-inne,
> With deop dich and derk · and dredful of siht[5].

Holy Church,

> A loveliche lady of lere · in lynnen y-clothid[6],

carries on with the Dreamer a conversation similar to the dialogues in morality plays[7]. There is, too, a conversation between the Dreamer and Scripture, and the personifications, Hunger and Fever, join them later[8]. Even the realistic figures of Wrath,

> with to white eyen,
> With a nyvylynge nose · nyppyng hus lyppes[9]

and Glutton are not unlike the comic characters introduced into the religious drama[10]. But the passage in which Langland's possible debt to the religious drama most clearly appears is the description of the Passion. Throughout these concluding cantos of the poem there are suggestions of a pageant or dramatic representation. Church music is heard in the vision;

> Of gurles and of *gloria laus* · gretliche me dremede,
> And how *osanna* by orgone · olde folk songe[11].

The chime of Easter bells and the Te Deum awaken the sleeper from the vision of the Redemption[12]. Skeat suggests that when relating Bible stories, besides supplementing the Gospel accounts

---

1 A I 15, X 18; B I 15, IX 19, XV 74; C II 15, XI 144, XVII 234.
2 B XIII 410; C VIII 70.   **3** B XIX 269; C XXII 274.   **4** A XI 106; B X 150, XIII 119; C XII 98.   **5** A P 12, cf. B P 12, C I 14.   **6** C II 3, cf. A I 3, B I 3.   **7** *Everyman*, dialogues between Everyman and Death, Fellowship, etc.   **8** A XII 63.   **9** C VII 103, cf. B V 135. **10** Wakefield Second Nativity Play; Chester Pageant of the Deluge. **11** C XXI 6, cf. B XVIII 8.   **12** B XVIII 422; C XXI 469.

with details from the apocryphal gospel of Nicodemus and from Grostête's *Castel of Love*, Langland continually had in his mind reminiscences of the Mysteries. Such details as the accusation of witchcraft brought against our Lord, and the name of Nicodemus, might have been found in the apocryphal gospel. But the story of Longinus was introduced from the *Aurea Legenda* into the miracle plays[1]. A dramatic performance possibly accounts for the appearance of Mercy and Truth, and later of Righteousness and Peace[2]:

> Out of the west coste · a wenche, as me thou3te,
> Cam walkynge in the wey · to-helle-ward she loked.
> Mercy hi3t that mayde · a meke thynge with-alle,
> A ful benygne buirde · and boxome of speche.
> Her suster, as it semed · cam softly walkynge,
> Evene out of the est · and westward she loked.
> A ful comely creature · Treuth she hi3te.

The account of the Harrowing of Hell[3] does net resemble the original story in the gospel of Nicodemus as closely as it does some of the miracle plays. The names of the devils and the dramatic account of their resistance might be derived from the latter[4]. A distinction is drawn between the Prince of Hell, Lucifer, and the Prince of Death, Satan, and to the former is assigned the temptation. Skeat points out several other instances in which Langland seems to have borrowed details of description and incident from these plays.

The splendid passage which depicts most vividly all that is pathetic and tragic in Christ's death also illustrates the limitations of contemporary biblical knowledge. Since simple highly coloured narratives were best remembered, authenticity was sacrificed to interest in the drama or in stained glass. Langland was following the custom of his predecessors when he described Christ

> in hus sorwe · on the selve rode,

as speaking the words:

> Bothe fox and fowel · may fleo to hole and crepe,
> And the fisshe hath fynnes · to flete with to reste,
> Ther Neode hath ynome me so · that ich mot neode abyde,
> And suffre sorwes soure · that shal to joye turne[5].

---

1 C xxi 90; see Skeat, note to C xxi 82, vol. ii.   2 B xviii 113, cf. C xxi 118; B xviii 166; C xxi 172.   3 B xviii 270; C xxi 297.
4 C xxi 283.   5 C xxiii 44, cf. B xx 43.

Besides the Longinus story there were many legends which had been adapted to contemporary taste and inserted into the popular accounts. Amongst those found in *Piers Plowman* are the legends of the salvation of Trajan[1], the Seven Sleepers[2], Mahomet's attempt to become Pope[3], the omen attending Constantine's gift to the Church[4], and the belief that the wood of the Cross was grown from the Apple from the Tree of Life[5].

The medieval inability to realise historical conditions, especially those of Eastern life, is most obvious in the pictorial representations which have come down to us. Perhaps it appears less plainly in *Piers Plowman* on account of the allegorical nature of the poem. Christ's entry into Jerusalem as a knight

> that cometh to be doubed,
> To geten hus gilte spores · and galoches y-couped[6],

was less remarkable when the Deadly Sins were peasants and merchants confessing to Repentance. Unfamiliar details in biblical stories were suppressed and replaced by homely phrases[7]. According to Langland's version of the parable[8], the Good Samaritan was journeying to a tournament at Jerusalem and " lyard," or " bayarde," bore him to a " graunge wel six myle or sevene biside the newe market." Faith, another traveller, would not approach the wounded man "by nyne londes lengthe," and Hope drew aside

> Dredfully, by this day! as duk · doth fram the faucoun.

This half-realistic, half-symbolic treatment of Bible stories[9], which is characteristic of medieval writers, sometimes cloaks their ignorance of the actual Bible text and proceeds at other times from the exaggerated importance which they attributed to the allegorical, as distinct from the literal, interpretation of Scripture. The general impression received from such passages of *Piers Plowman* is that clerical knowledge of biblical stories, especially of those which lent themselves to pictorial or dramatic representation, covered a fairly wide field but was not remarkably accurate. Occasionally very obvious inaccuracies occur; the wise sayings of other men are attributed to Solomon,

---

1 B xi 136; C xiii 75.   2 B xiv 68; C xvi 272.   3 B xv 389; C xviii 165.   4 B xv 519; C xviii 220.   5 B xviii 140; C xxi 144. 6 C xxi 11, cf. B xviii 13.   7 B xii 147, xv 455; C xv 90.   8 B xvii 48; C xx 47.   9 See Wyclif, i 33, Sermon xiii.

and Nebuchadnezzar is mentioned when Belshazzar should be[1]. But Langland appears to have been fairly well acquainted with the text of the Scriptures after the fashion of his time, though he quotes little that is not in the Breviary, and confuses the sixth with the seventh commandment. He is himself ever ready with a text or an illustration from the Bible and urges[2] the ecclesiastics to improve their knowledge of it:

> For goddis worde wolde nou3t be loste · for that worcheth evere,
> If it availled nou3t the comune · it my3te availle 3owselven[3].

1 A III 84, VIII 139; B III 93, VII 153, cf. C x 306; B XI 245, 262, 265; C IV 121.   2 B XI 300; C XIV 121.   3 B X 272.

VII

MEDIEVAL WOMEN

THE testimony of *Piers Plowman* regarding women suggests that, in spite of a general inclination to depreciate feminine ability, women of every class managed to share in the government of home, town and country. The poet suggests that women's inability to keep their own counsel unfitted them to take part in political or ecclesiastical work[1]. The details recorded by him of the part played by women do not consistently prove his statements. The sphere of the medieval woman seems to have been far wider than that assigned to her by ecclesiastical or chivalrous ideals.

Though certain women were exalted amongst the saints of the Church, the general tendency in ecclesiastical circles was to regard woman as the accomplice of the devil. Marriage was regarded as a confession of failure, since the titles "Virgin" and "Martyr" were most desirable. The poet's recollections of women dedicated to religion did not support the theory of the superiority of celibacy[2]. Though he repeated the orthodox statements on marriage[3] he profited by practical experience, and took for his ideal reformer a married man who paid a high tribute to his good wife by leaving her in charge of his worldly property[4]. This was probably the attitude of the average layman; he acquiesced in the ecclesiastical conventions, but his actions were mainly guided by common sense.

Similarly the chivalrous romance represented woman either as a half-divine being whose only duty was to exert a gracious influence over the knight, or as an enchantress by whose machinations the hero was deceived and outwitted. In reality the medieval lady frequently administered the affairs of her estates[5], borrowed money from usurers, and preferred the performances

---

1 B v 168, xix 157; C xxii 162.   2 B v 157; C vii 132.   3 B xvi 71; C xix 89.   4 A vii 89; B vi 98; C ix 105.   5 B v 247; C vii 249.

of minstrels and "jogelours[1]" to the more becoming occupation of embroidering Church vestments with her "longe fyngres[2]."

A highborn lady shared many of the landowner's responsibilities and pleasures. Besides receiving outward signs of respect[3], she frequently governed her estate. Langland considered it necessary to warn ladies as well as lords of the evils of disinheriting their heirs in favour of the regular clergy[4]. The description of Lady Mede, which in the later versions is supposed to have been based on the character of Alice Perrers, illustrates the power an unscrupulous woman might exercise in higher spheres of life. The poet describes her as

> a womman · wortheli yclothed,
> Purfiled with pelure · the finest upon erthe,
> Y-crounede with a corone · the kyng hath non better.
> Fetislich hir fyngres · were fretted with golde wyre,
> And there-on red rubyes · as red as any glede,
> And diamantz of derrest pris · and double manere safferes,
> Orientales and ewages · envenymes to destroye.
> Hire robe was ful riche · of red scarlet engreyned,
> With ribanes of red golde · and of riche stones;
> Hire arraye me ravysshed · suche ricchesse saw I nevere;
> I had wondre what she was · and whas wyf she were[5].

With such attractions, natural and artificial, she exercised her cunning and plausibility to the greatest advantage. Though her knowledge of Latin, the basis of a medieval education, was negligible, she bewildered king and court with her arguments and made them waver in their decision.

The middle-class woman was unaffected by chivalrous ideals, and probably seldom contemplated the possibility of attaining to heaven's greatest reward. According to Langland's account, she was her own mistress in workroom or tavern[6]; cheating her employees or customers and increasing her profits and custom as she pleased[7]. Every privilege was jealously guarded and envied. "Letice at the style," who received the holy bread first of the wives and widows sitting in the pews[8], was drawn into a violent quarrel after the meal later in the day, by a rival who had not

---

1 B xiii 422; C viii 82, x 130.   2 A vii 18; B vi 10; C ix 9; Langlois, *Moralistes*, 27, Etienne de Fougères, *Le livre des Manières*.   3 B xv 6.
4 B xv 316; C xviii 55.   5 B ii 8, cf. A ii 8; C iii 9; *Knight of La Tour Landry*, E.E.T.S., Wright, pp. 39, 65, 69; Wyclif, "Confessio derelicti Pauperis," xth commandment.   6 A v 129; B v 215; C vii 221.
7 A v 133, 148; B v 219, 306; C vii 225, 353.   8 C vii 145.

dared to disturb the congregation by pressing before her at mass. The beauty of Eleyne's new cloak prevented her neighbour from concentrating her attention on the service[1]. Langland, with a mature moralist's sensitiveness to the evil effects of this passion for dress, besought women to pack away their finery in the family chest in readiness for a time of need[2]. He ridicules Watte, who gave but a groat for his own hood, whilst his wife wore a headdress worth a mark or a noble[3].

An account is given of the attempt made in the poorest homes "to turne the fayre outwarde"; the chief burden seems to have fallen on the mothers who

> That thei with spynnynge may spare · spenen hit in hous-hyre,
> Bothe in mylk and in mele · to make with papelotes,
> To a-glotye with here gurles · that greden after fode.
> Al-so hem-selve · suffren muche hunger,
> And wo in winter-tyme · with wakynge a nyghtes
> To ryse to the ruel · to rocke the cradel,
> Bothe to karde and to kembe · to clouten and to wasche,
> To rubbe and to rely · russhes to pilie,
> That reuthe is to rede · othere in ryme shewe
> The wo of these women · that wonyeth in cotes[4].

All housewives found sufficient employment for their energies in spinning or weaving[5]. The peasant's wife made pottage for the labourers and sewed wheat-sacks[6]. The rare occasions on which a woman donned her veil and left her house to go on a pilgrimage must have been for her times of great excitement and pleasure rather than penance[7].

It is possible that, during the pestilence, the materialistic spirit of the age destroyed any beneficial influence which chivalry might have exercised on woman's status in the upper classes, or on the Church's conditional consecration of marriage for all classes. According to Langland, marriage was regarded as a purely business arrangement[8], and, though this was no novelty in the later fourteenth century, it is possible that it was accentuated during those hard years when wealth was the first object with many men. Women were regarded as mere chattels, entitling their owners to a certain amount of property. Land-

---

1 A v 91; B v 110.   **2** A v 26; B v 26; C vi 129, cf. A iv 102; B iv 116; C v 111.   **3** A v 30; B v 30; C vi 133.   **4** C x 74.   **5** A vii 13; B vi 13; C ix 12.   **6** A vii 9; B vi 9; C ix 8, 182.   **7** A vii 7; B vi 7; C ix 5.   **8** A x 177, 191; B ix 155, 171; C xi 257, 279.

owners arranged their children's marriages with a view to acquiring further possessions[1]. Squires and knights sought wealth rather than beauty, birth or manners[2]. Young girls married old men, and rich widows were married for the sake of their property[3]. Marriages were arranged by agents[4]; and, where great wealth was concerned, the king and his ministers intervened to prevent their enemies from annexing it[5]. The necessity of possessing a dowry gave rise to charities which provided for portionless girls[6].

On these occasions when great wealth was concerned, the marriage ceremony was performed with much splendour[7]; and relatives and friends of both bride and bridegroom travelled long distances to witness the signing of charters endowing the bride with her property[8]. When the company could not be accommodated in hall or house, tents and pavilions were erected[9]. After the bridal celebrations, the married couple frequently spent the rest of their lives in quarrelling; and the poet suggested

Thauh thei don hem to Donemowe · bote the devel hem helpe
To folwen for the flicche · feccheth thei hit nevere;
Bote thei bothe be for-swore · that bacon thei tyne[10].

In theory, divorce found no place in Church law; a couple once legally married could never be separated. But the complexities of Canon Law, with its strange mixture of unreasonable severity and unreasonable licence, afforded a thousand opportunities of proving that the marriage had never been legal; and it was as easy for rich folk to shake off the bond by pleading nullity of marriage as it is for their modern descendants to escape by divorce. Moreover, common sense, in the fourteenth century, often brushed aside the legal fictions and called things by their true names. Langland attributes the frequency of divorce to the corruption of ecclesiastical courts. Referring to the court of consistory, he says they

matrimoigne for monye · maken and unmaken,
And that conscience and Cryst · hath yknitte faste,
Thei undon it unworthily · tho doctours of lawe[11].

1 C xi 256.   2 B ii 75; C iii 80, xi 260.   3 A x 180; B ix 160.
4 B xiv 267; C xvii 109.   5 A iii 105; B ii 65, iii 109; C iii 66,
iv 146.   6 A viii 31; B vii 29; C x 33; Toulmin Smith, *English Gilds*, p. 194; Ludlow, *Gild of the Palmers*.   7 A ii 36; B ii 54; C ii 55.
8 A ii 58; B ii 72; C iii 73, iv 372.   9 A ii 40, 44.   10 C xi 276,
cf. A x 188, B ix 168.   11 B xv 236.

And he describes how easily Covetousness, in the Court of Arches, for a miniver mantle, made

> leel matrimonye
> Departe er deth come · and a devors shupte[1].

In humbler walks of life the experience that a disobedient wife was one of

> Thre thinges... · that doth a man by strengthe
> Forto fleen his owne hous[2]

had resulted in the institution of public punishments for contumacious helpmates. Thomas Stowe[3] was advised to arm himself with two rods before he dispersed the crowd and brought his wife home. Yet Langland, with a touch of humour, showed that diplomacy was sometimes resorted to as the best policy in dealing with a shrew. Dame Study's husband before her

> bicome so confus · he couth noüʒte loke,
> And as doumbe as deth · and drowe hym arrere[4].

As he explained to his guest, such humility flattered his wife, and was the surest means of calming her anger[5]. The noble lord enforced obedience on his lady by guarding her in a castle[6].

We may possibly trace the harmful effect of the pestilence on family life in Langland's exhortations to parents; but he, like other contemporaries, attributes the plague to the already pre-existing sins of the world. He traced the lack of discipline to the parents' indulgence of children whom they feared to lose[7]. It must be noted, however, that this particular complaint is of all times and all places; nor can we assume that Langland would not have written exactly in the same strain even though he had never lived to see the Black Death.

We must here conclude our study of this poem, one of the most truly national in all English literature, and one of the richest mines for students of social history. It has been impossible, within our necessary limits, to give much more than a bare *catalogue raisonné* of Langland's evidence, by the aid of which

---

1 C xxiii 136, cf. B xx 135.   2 B xvii 316, cf. C xx 297.   3 A v 28; B v 28; C vi 131.   4 B x 136, cf. A xi 93.   5 A xi 97; B x 140; C xii 86.   6 A x 10; B ix 10; C xi 136.   7 A iv 103, v 32; B iv 117, v 34; C v 112, vi 137.

and of our Index future students may find it easier to exploit
this testimony to the full. Yet the author ventures to hope that
even such a bare summary may appeal to a few general readers
also, since it needs no great effort of imagination to clothe the
skeleton in the flesh and blood, and to see behind these jejune
details some of the realities which stirred men to passion, to
hope or to despair in one of the most living periods of English
history.

APPENDIX

LIST OF BIBLE REFERENCES

THIS list includes such references to Holy Scripture as are either obvious or have been pointed out by Skeat. In assigning the references to book, chapter and verse, the order of the Vulgate version has been followed. Italicized references are those of passages quoted by the author not in English but in the Latin of the Vulgate. Square brackets indicate that Langland's words vaguely suggest a Scriptural phrase or passage.

Genesis
  i 26—*A x 41.*
  i 31—*B xi 388.*
  [ii 12—A xi 12; B x 12.]
  ii 17—B xviii 193; C xxi 201.
  [iii 3—B xv 61; C xvii 223.]
  iii 19—*A vii 220 ff.; B vi 235 ff.; C ix 242 ff.*
  vi 6, 7—*A x 156; B ix 129; C xi 221.*
  xii 2—B xvi 239; C xix 257.
  xii 7, 8—B xvi 244; C xix 263.
  xiii 16—B xvi 239; C xix 257.
  xiii 18—B xvi 244; C xix 263.
  [xiv 18—B xvi 244; C xix 263.]
  xv 5-16—B xvi 239; C xix 257.
  xvii 23—B xvi 235; C xix 253.
  xviii 1—B xvi 225; C xix 242.
  xviii 7, 8—B xvi 229.
  xviii 10—C xix 246.
  xviii 17, 18—B xvi 239; C xix 257.
  xix 32—*B i 31; C ii 30.*
  xx 2 ff.—C xiv 10.
  xxii 2—B xvi 231; C xix 249.
  [xxx 23—B xvi 219; C xix 224.]
  xxxvii 9, 10—A viii 145; B vii 159; C x 308.
Exodus
  x 17—*B xx 276; C xxiii 278.*
  xx 12—*B v 576; C viii 216, xviii 58.*
  xx 13—A xi 247; B x 368, *xix 443; C xxii 448.*
  xxi 24—*B xviii 337; C xxi 388.*
Leviticus
  xi 3—B xv 458.
  xix 13—*C iv 310.*

Leviticus (*continued*)
  [xix 15—B xv 86; C xvii 240.]
  xix 17—*B xi 87, 90; C xiii 33.*
  xix 18—C vi 58.
  [xxv 10—B x 320; C vi 172.]
Numbers
  xx 11—B xiv 63; C xvi 267.
Deuteronomy
  [i 17—B xv 86; C xvii 240.]
  vi 5—B i 149.
  viii 3—*B xiv 46; C xvi 246.*
  viii 15—B xiv 63; C xvi 268.
  x 12—B i 149.
  xii 6—*B xv 518; C xviii 219.*
  [xvi 19—B xv 86; C xvii 240.]
  xxiii 25—*B xv 558; C xviii 280.*
  xxxii 35—*A xi 247; B vi 228, x 369, xix 443; C xxii 448.*
1 Kings (1 Samuel)
  [i 6—B xvi 219; C xix 224.]
  iv 11—C i 104.
  iv 11, 18—B x 280.
  xv—A iii 244 ff.; B iii 257 ff.; C iv 412 ff.
  xviii 7—*B xix 131; C xxii 135.*
  [xxii 2—A i 96; B i 102; C ii 102.]
2 Kings (2 Samuel)
  xi 14, 15—A xi 280; B x 423; C xii 265.
  xviii—C iv 410.
3 Kings (1 Kings)
  iii 26—*C xii 215.*
1 Paralipomenon (Chronicles)
  [xi 1-3—A i 96; B i 102; C ii 102.]
  [xii 17, 18—A i 96; B i 102; C ii 102.]

Tobias

ii 21—*C xviii 40.*

[iii 6—C ii 144, vii 290, xviii 40.]

[iii 22—B xviii 406; C xxi 454.]

iv 9—*B x 86; C xii 71.*

Job

ii 10—*C xiv 17.*

vi 5—*B xv 312; C xviii 52.*

vii 9—B xviii 149; C xxi 153.

x 22—B xx 268; C xxiii 270.

xv 34—*A iii 86;* B *iii 95;* C *iv 123.* Wrongly attributed to Solomon.

xxi 7—*A xi 23; B x 25.*

xxi 13—*C xii 24.*

Psalms

i 1—*B v 425, xiii 53.*

i 6—B x 321.

iv 3—*B xv 79.*

iv 9—*B xv 249, xviii 184;* C *xxi 192.*

v 7—*C xxi 359.*

vi 7—*B xv 186; C xvii 330.*

vii 15—*A x 145;* B *ix 121;* C *xi 211.*

vii 16—*B xviii 358.*

[vii 16—B xviii 160; C xxi 166, 395.]

ix 2—*B xiii 55.*

ix 7—*B xiii 331; C vii 76.*

[ix 16—B xviii 16; C xxi 166, 395.]

xiii 1—*B vii 135.*

xiii 3—*B iv 35, 36; C v 36.*

xiv 1—*B ii 38, iii 233, vii 51, xiii 126; C iii 39, xvi 135.*

xiv 2—*B iii 236.*

xiv 5—*A iii 227, viii 47, 55;* B *iii 240, vi 41;* C *iii 40.*

xv 5—*B xii 189; C vi 60, xv 129.*

xvii 26—*B v 285, xix 420; C xxii 424.*

xviii 1—*C xix 215.*

xix 8, 9—*B x 322; C vi 173.*

xxii 4—*A viii 101, x 86;* B *vii 116, xii 13, 289.*

xxiii 9—*B xviii 259; C xxi 272.*

xxv 10—*A iii 233;* B *iii 247;* C *iv 118.*

xxix 6—*B xviii 179; C xxi 185.*

xxx 11—*C x 162.*

xxxi 1—*B v 515, xii 178, xiii 53, 54, xiv 93; C viii 153, xv 117.*

[xxxi 5—B xi 81.]

xxxi 6—*B xiii 57; C xvi 61.*

Psalms (*continued*)

xxxiii 11—A viii 108; B vii 123, *ix 106, xi 273;* C *xi 201.*

xxxiii 20—A viii 107; B vii 122.

xxxv 7—*B x 410; C xii 250.*

xxxv 7, 8—*B v 516; C viii 154.*

xxxvi 3—*B xi 278, xv 175; C xiv 101.*

xxxvi 4—C xvi 275.

xxxvi 24—*B xvi 25.*

xxxvi 25—*B vii 88, xi 270;* C *x 162.*

xxxvii 1—*C xxi 437.*

xxxviii 2—B xiii 55.

xxxviii 7—*C xiii 215.*

[xxxix 6—B x 44.]

xli 4—*A viii 108; B vii 123.*

xlii 1—*B xi 277.*

xlvi 2—B xviii 405; C xxi 452.

xlvi 8—*B xi 302; C xiv 123.*

xlviii 20—*C xii 25.*

xlix 21—*B x 285, xi 91;* C *xiii 30.*

l 3—*B xiii 52.*

l 6—*B xviii 376; C xxi 423.*

l 8—*B v 283; C vii 303.*

l 9—*C xvii 332.*

l 19—*B xiii 58, xv 188; C xvi 62, xvii 333.*

lvi 5—*B xiii 331; C vii 76.*

lxi 13—*B xii 213; C vi 32, xv 153.*

lxvii 19—*B v 498; C viii 131.*

lxviii 29—*A vii 68, 69;* B *vi 77, 78; C ix 77, 78.*

lxx 15—*A viii 122.*

lxx 20—*B v 514; C viii 152.*

lxxii 12—*B x 26; C xii 25.*

lxxii 20—*B xiv 130; C xvi 310.*

lxxv 6—*B xiv 130; C xvi 310.*

lxxx 13—*B ix 65; C xi 164.*

lxxxiv 11—B xviii 115, *421;* C xxi 120, *468.*

xcvi 7—*B xv 79.*

c 7—*B xiii 433; C viii 93.*

civ 15—*B xii 127; C xv 69.*

cix 1—*C ii 122.*

cx 3—*C xviii 65.*

cx 10—*A x 81;* B *ix 93.*

cxi 1—*B v 425, xiii 53.*

cxi 5—*B v 246.*

cxi 9—*B xv 320.*

cxviii 158—*A xii 19.*

cxxvii 1—*A vii 237;* B *v 425, vi 252.*

cxxvii 2—*A vii 237;* B *vi 254; C ix 262.*

Psalms (*continued*)

cxxxi 6—*A xi 55*; B *x 68, xv 482*; C *xii 51*.

cxxxii 1—*A xi 189*; B *xviii 423*; C *xxi 470*.

[cxxxiv 6—B xii 216; C xv 156.]

cxxxvii 1—*B xiii 55*.

cxlii 2—*B xviii 397*; C *xxi 444*.

cxliv 9—*B v 289, xi 134, xvii 312*; C *xiii 73, xx 294*. Not exact.

cxliv 16—*B xiv 62*; C *xvi 266, xvii 317*.

cxlvi 4—*B xx 255*; C *xxiii 256*.

cxlviii 5—*A x 34*; B *ix 32, xiv 59*; C *xv 166, xvi 264*.

Proverbs

i 7—*A x 81*; B *ix 93*.

iii 12—B xii 12.

iv 23—A x 45; B ix 23, 55; C xi 148, 173.

ix 10—*A x 81*; B *ix 93*.

[x 19—B xi 406; C xiv 226.]

x 26—B xvii 315; C xx 297.

xiii 24—*B v 39*; C *vi 140*.

[xvii 14—B xvi 43; C xix 46.]

[xvii 28—B xi 406; C xiv 226.]

xix 13—B xvii 315; C xx 297.

xx 4—A vii 223; B vi 238; C *ix 246*. Wrongly referred to Sapience.

xxii 1—*B iii 327*; C *iv 485*.

xxii 9—*B iii 332, 346*; C *iv 489* (not in Wisdom), *499*.

xxii 10—*A viii 126*; B *vii 137*.

xxiv 16—*A ix 16*; B *viii 21*; C *xi 21*.

[xxiv 16—B xv 86; C xvii 240.]

xxv 17—*B xv 54*; C *xvii 216*.

xxv 22—B xiii 144; C xvi 143.

xxvii 15—B xvii 315; C xx 207.

xxx 8—*B xi 262*. Not of Solomon.

Ecclesiastes

iv 10—*C xxi 318*.

ix 1—*B x 430*; C *xii 273*.

x 16—B p 191; C i 205.

Ecclesiasticus

i 16—*A x 81*; B *ix 93*.

v 5—*B xii 207*; C *xv 147*.

x 10—*B x 337*.

xi 9—*B xi 9*; C *xiv 198*.

xxix 27—A i 20; B i 20; C ii 20.

xxxi 8—*B xv 229*; C *xvii 356*.

[xxxviii 2—A viii 47; B vi 43.]

[xlii 1—B xv 86; C xvii 240.]

Isaiah

ii 4—*B iii 306, 322*; C *iv 464, 480*.

iii 7—*B xv 567*.

v 22—*B xiii 61*; C *xvi 65*.

ix 2—*B v 501*; C *viii 134*.

xiv 4, 5, 6—*B x 328*; C *vi 178*.

[xiv 13, 14—B i 117; C ii 111.]

[xiv 14—B xv 51; C xvii 213.]

xxx 15—*B xiv 180*.

xl 12—B xvii 138; C xx 112.

xlv 24—B xix 16; C xxii 16.

lv 1—*B xi 115*; C *xiii 56*.

lvi 10—*B x 287*.

lviii 7—*B x 82*; C *x 125, xii 67*.

Jeremiah

xxxi 34—*C viii 148*.

Ezechiel

xvi 49—B xiv 76; C xvi 231.

xviii 20—*B ix 144, x 110*; C *xi 235*. Not the Gospel.

xxxiii 11—C xv 135.

Daniel

ii 39—Cf. A viii 139; cf. B vii 153; C x 306.

v 28—Cf. A viii 139; cf. B vii 153; C x 306.

ix 24—B xviii 109; C xxi 114.

ix 24, 26—B xv 589.

Hosea

xiii 3—A vi 102; B v 622; C viii 265.

xiii 14—*B xvii 111, xviii 35*; C *xxi 34*.

Joel

iii 2, 12, 13—B xviii 367; C xxi 414.

Zacharias

xiii 7—*C x 261*.

Malachias

iii 10—*B xv 568*. Not Hosea.

S. Matthew

i 18—C xiii 133.

ii 1—*B xii 145*; C *xv 88*.

ii 2, 9—B xviii 231; C xxi 243.

ii 11—B xix 72; C xxii 76.

iii 2—*B xiii 48*; C *xvi 56*.

[iii 11—B xii 282; C xv 207.]

iv 4—*B xiv 46*; C *vi 86, xvi 246*.

iv 18—B xv 287; C xviii 19.

v 3—*B xiv 214*.

v 13—*B xv 421, 423*.

v 17—*B xviii 347*; C *xxi 398*.

v 19—*A xi 193*; B *xiii 117*; C *xvi 127*.

v 21—A xi 247; B x 368.

S. Matthew (*continued*)

v 45—*B xix 429*; *C xxii 433*.

vi 2, 5, 16—*A iii 65, 239*; *B iii 252*; *C iv 314*.

vi 3—*A iii 55*; *B iii 72*; *C iv 74*.

vi 10—*B xiv 48, xv 174*; *C vi 88, xvi 251, xvii 318*.

vi 11—*C xvii 371*.

vi 12—*B xix 392*; *C xxii 396*.

vi 16—*B xv 213*; *C xvii 341*.

vi 21—B xiii 399; C vii 285

vi 24—A ix 81; B viii 89, xiii 313; *C vii 60*, xi 87.

vi 25—*A viii 112*; *B vii 126*, though S. Luke is mentioned.

vi 25, 26—*B xiv 33*.

vii 1—*B xi 88, xii 91, xiv 290*; *C xiii 31, xvii 128*.

vii 2—*A i 150*; *B i 176, xi 221* (not S. John); *C ii 175, xii 234*.

vii 3—*B x 262*.

vii 5—*B x 264*.

vii 6—*A xi 9*; *B x 9*; *C xii 7*.

vii 7—*B xv 420, 494*.

vii 12—*B vii 61*; *C xvii 306*.

vii 16, 17—*B ix 150*; *C xi 244*.

vii 17—*B ii 27*; *C iii 29*.

vii 18—C xi 206.

vii 21—*B xvii 262*; *C xx 228*.

vii 23—*B v 56*.

viii 20—B xx 43; C xxiii 44.

[ix 4—B xv 194; C xvii 337.]

ix 12—*B xvi 110*.

ix 13—*B v 506*; *C viii 139*.

x 10—*A ii 90*; *B ii 122*.

x 22—*B xiii 49*; *C xvi 57*.

[x 22—B xiii 134, 171, xiv 33, 52, xv 262, 581; C xvi 138, 157, 255.]

x 28—*C xi 98*.

[x 42—C x 124.]

xi 5—*C xix 142*.

[xi 5—B xix 121; C xxii 125.]

xii 23—*B xix 129*; *C xxii 133*.

xiii 44—*C vi 98*.

xiv 17, 20—B xvi 125; C xix 154.

xiv 17, 21—B xix 122; C xxii 126.

xiv 25—C xxi 252.

xiv 28—*B xviii 242*; *C xxi 255*.

xv 14—*B x 276* (referred to S. Mark), *xii 185*; *C xv 125* (referred to S. Luke).

[xvi 18—B xv 206.]

xvi 19—*A viii 162*; B p 101, *vii 175*; C i 129, *x 326*.

xvi 27—*B xii 213*; *C xv 153*.

S. Matthew (*continued*)

xvii 19—*B xi 272*.

xviii 3—*B xv 145*; *C xvii 296*.

xviii 7—*A xi 151*; *B xvi 157*; *C xix 176*.

xix 21—*B xi 265* (not S. Luke); *C xiii 166*.

[xix 24—B xiv 144.]

xix 24—*B xiv 211*, cf. C xvii 54; *C xii 203*.

[xix 29—B xiv 264; C xvii 106.]

xix 29—*C xiii 159*.

xx 4, 7—*B x 474, xv 491*.

xx 11—B xiv 144.

xxi 9—*B xviii 15, 17*; *C xxi 13, 15*.

xxi 12—*C xix 159*.

xxi 13—*B xvi 135*, cf. C xix 160.

xxii 1–13—B xi 107; C xiii 46.

xxii 4—*B xv 456*.

xxii 20, 21—*A i 49*, cf. *B. i 52*; *C ii 48*.

xxii 37, 39—*A xi 236*; *B xiii 126*, cf. *C xvi 135*.

xxii 40—*B xvii 13*; *C xx 15*.

xxiii 2—*A xi 219*; *B x 398*; *C ix 86, xii 237*.

xxiii 3—*C ix 90*.

xxiii 27—B xv 112; C xvii 268.

xxv 12—*B ix 65, xvii 249*; *C xx 215*.

xxv 14 ff.—A vii 225; B vi 240; C ix 247.

xxv 23—C xv 214.

[xxv 35—C x 124.]

xxv 46—*A viii 95*; *B vii 111*; *C x 287*.

xxvi 5—*C xix 166*.

xxvi 7—B xiii 194.

xxvi 15—B xvi 143; C xix 166.

xxvi 25—*B xvi 145*.

xxvi 48—B xvi 147.

xxvi 49—*B xvi 151*; *C xix 170*.

xxvi 57, 59—B xix 136; C xxii 140.

xxvi 60, 61—B xviii 40; C xxi 39.

xxvi 61—C xix 163.

[xxvii 19—B xviii 298.]

xxvii 19—*B xviii 36*; *C xxi 35*.

xxvii 22—*B xviii 39*; *C xxi 38*.

xxvii 29—*B xviii 47*; *C xxi 49*.

xxvii 29, 30—B xviii 50; C xxi 50.

xxvii 40, 42—B xviii 54; C xxi 54.

xxvii 45, 51, 52—B xviii 60–63; C xxi 61–64.

xxvii 46—*B xvi 214*.

xxvii 54—*B xviii 68*; *C xxi 71*.

S. Matthew (*continued*)

xxvii 63—B xvii 109.

xxvii 64, 66—B xix 139; C xxii 143.

xxviii 4—B xix 145; C xxii 149.

xxviii 13—B xix 149; C xxii 154.

xxviii 19—B xv 482.

xxviii 48—B xviii 52; C xxi 52.

S. Mark

ii 17—*B xvi 110.*

iii 29—*B xvii 197; C xx 162.*

vi 38, 43—B xvi 125; C xix 154.

vi 38, 44—B xix 122; C xxii 126.

[vii 32, 37—B xix 126; C xxii 130.]

viii 31—B xvii 109.

x 18—*C xvi 136.*

x 48—*B xix 129; C xxii 133.*

xi 15—*C xix 159.*

xi 17—*B xvi 135,* cf. C xix 160.

xi 18—B xvi 136.

xii 42—B xiii 196.

xii 43—*C xiv 98.*

xiii 9, 11—*A xi 287; B x 443; C xii 277.*

xiv 3—B xiii 194.

xiv 11—C xix 166.

xiv 37, 38—C x 257.

xiv 44—B xvi 147.

xiv 45—*B xvi 151; C xix 170.*

xiv 58—B xvi 131; C xix 161, 163.

xv 17—B xviii 47; C xxi 47.

xv 34—B xvi 214.

xv 36—B xviii 52; C xxi 52.

xv 39—*B xviii 68; C xxi 71.*

xvi 15—B xv 482, *483; C xviii 191.*

xvi 16—*A xi 229,* cf. B x 346 (rather than S. Peter or S. Paul); *B xi 119; C xiii 58, xiv 87.*

xvi 17, 18—*B xiii 249; C xvi 222.*

S. Luke[1]

[i 25—B xvi 219; C xix 224.]

i 26—B xvi 90; C xix 124.

i 38—*B xvi 99; C xix 133.*

i 52—*B xv 514; C xviii 215.*

i 55—B xvi 239, *242;* C xix 257.

i 68—*C xvi 117.*

ii 14—*B xii 151, xix 70; C xv 94, xxii 74.*

ii 15—*B xii 143; C xv 86.*

v 31—*B xvi 110.*

vi 25—*B xiii 424; C viii 84.*

S. Luke (*continued*)

vi 37—*B xii 91.*

vi 38—*A i 150, 175; B i 176, 199, xi 221* (not S. John), *xii 56; C ii 175, 197.*

vi 39—*B x 276* (not S. Mark), *xii 185; C xv 125.*

vi 41—*B x 262.*

vi 42—*B x 264.*

vii 20—C xviii 313.

vii 36, 48, 50—B xi 211.

vii 37—B xiii 194.

viii 3—C xix 97.

viii 21—A i 89; B i 91; C ii 87.

ix 13, 14—B xix 122; C xxii 126.

ix 16, 17—B xvi 125; C xix 155.

ix 58—B xx 43; C xxiii 44.

x 4—*C x 123.*

x 7—*A ii 90; B ii 122, xiii 39; C xvi 45.*

x 16—*B xiii 441; C viii 101* (referred to S. John).

x 27—*B xv 574, xvii 11; C xx 13.*

x 30—*B xvii 55; C xx 55.*

x 33—B xvii 48; C xx 47.

x 40—*B xi 243; C xiii 136.*

x 42—*B xi 246; C xiii 139.*

xi 15—B xvi 120; C xix 151.

[xi 17—B xv 194; C xvii 337.]

xi 19—B xvi 121.

xii 20—*C xiii 215.*

xii 22—*A viii 112; B vii 126, xiv 33.*

xii 27—*B v 56.*

xii 38—*B xii 9.*

xii 47, 48—*B xii 58; C xv 18.*

xiv 10—*B vi 49; C ix 44.*

xiv 11—*A x 115.*

xiv 12—*B xi 185; C xiii 102.*

[xiv 12—B xv 86; C xvii 240.]

xiv 18–20—C viii 292.

xiv 20—*B xiv 3.*

xiv 33—*C xiii 170.*

xv 9—*C vi 98.*

xvi 9—*A vii 215; B vi 230; C ix 235.*

xvi 9, 13—A ix 81; B viii 89; C xi 87.

xvi 9—*C xx 246.*

xvi 10–13—A i 89; B i 91; C ii 87.

xvi 19—B xiv 122, xvii 263; C xvi 303, xx 230, *236.*

---

[1] The vague "Luke bereth witnesse" of B x 73 may be here mentioned in a footnote.

S. Luke (*continued*)
xvi 22—B xvi 255; C xix 273.
[xviii 7—B xi 368; C xiv 197.]
xviii 20—*B xix 443; C xxii 448.*
xviii 38—*B xix 129; C xxii 133.*
xix 8—*B xiii 195.*
xix 23—*B vii 83.*
xix 47—B xvi 137.
xxi 2—B xiii 196.
xxi 3—C xiv 98.
xxii 5—C xix 166.
xxii 21, 22—B xvi 142.
xxii 35—*C x 120.*
xxiii 42—A v 247; B v 474; C vii 321.
xxiii 56—C xix 97.
xxiv 13—B xi 226; C xiii 122.
[xxiv 39—B xviii 302; C xxi 340.]
xxiv 46—*B xix 156; C xxii 161.*
S. John
i 14—*B v 508; C iv 358, viii 141.*
i 29—*B xvi 252; C xix 270.*
ii 2—B ix 117.
ii 9—B xix 104; C xxii 108.
ii 15—B xvi 128.
ii 19—*C xix 162.*
ii 21—C xix 164.
iii 5—*B xi 82.*
iii 8—*B xii 65, 71; C xv 27.*
iii 11—*B xii 67.*
iii 13—*A xi 255; B x 377; C xii 209.*
vi 9, 10—B xix 122; C xxii 126.
vi 9, 13—B xvi 125; C xix 154.
viii 7—*C xv 42,* cf. B xii 80.
viii 34—*B xi 197; C xiii 111.*
viii 48, 52—*B xvi 120; C xix 151.*
x 11—*B xv 489; C xviii 193, 293.*
x 16—*C xix 266.*
x 38—*C xvii 339.*
xi 33—B xvi 115; C xix 146.
xi 39—*B xvi 114; C xviii 305, xix 145.*
xi 43—*B xv 584.*
xii 3—B xiii 194.
xii 24—*C xiii 178.*
xii 31—*B xviii 312; C xxi 352.*
xii 32—*B xvii 149; C xx 125.*
xiv 6—*B ix 159; C xi 255.*
xiv 9, 10—Cf. B v 494; *B x 244; C viii 129, xii 156.*
xiv 13—*B xiv 46; C xvi 246.*
xvi 11—*A x 8, 62; B ix 8; C xi 134.*
xvi 20—*C xiii 207.*

S. John (*continued*)
xvi 23—*C viii 260.*
[xvii 2—B xii 289.]
xviii 8—*C xix 178.*
xviii 38—*A xii 28.*
xix 2—B xviii 47; C xxi 49.
xix 15—B xviii 46; C xxi 46.
[xix 23, 24—C xi 193.]
xix 28—*C xxi 411.*
xix 30—*B xviii 57; C xxi 58.*
xix 32—B xviii 73; C xxi 76.
xix 34—B xviii 78; C xxi 81.
xx 14—B xix 152; C xxii 157.
xx 26—B xix 160, *164*; C xxii 165, *169*.
xx 28—*B xix 167; C xxii 172.*
xx 29—*B xix 176; C xxii 181.*
Acts
ii 1–4—B xix 196; C xxii 201.
ii 3—B xii 283; C xv 208.
iii 6—*B xiii 255; C xvi 226.*
xviii 3—Cf. B xv 285; C xviii 17.
xx 35—*C xv 16.*
xxiii 3—B xv 112; C xvii 268.
Romans
iv 11—B xvi 247; C xix 267.
iv 13—B xvi 239; C xix 257.
[xii 3—C xvii 227.]
xii 15—*A xi 190.*
xii 19—*A xi 247; B vi 228, x 204, 369, xix 443; C xviii 235* (not S. Luke), *xxii 448.*
xii 20—B xiii 144; C xvi 143.
xiii 7—*A v 242; B v 469; C vii 316.*
xiv 11—B xix 16; C xxii 16.
1 Corinthians
iii 18—*C x 127.*
iii 19—*B xii 140; C xv 83.*
vii 2—*B ix 191; C xi 296.*
vii 9—B ix 176; C xi 284.
vii 20—*A x 108; C vi 43.*
viii 1—*B xii 59.*
[x 4—B xv 206.]
xii 4—*B xix 223; C xxii 228.*
xiii 1—*B xvii 257; C xx 223.*
xiii 4, 5—*B xv 152; C xvii 289.*
xiii 7—*C xviii 5.*
xiii 12—*B xv 157; C xvii 294.*
xiii 13—*B xii 30.*
2 Corinthians
vi 10—*C xiv 4.*
xi 19—*A ix 83; B viii 91; C xi 89.*
xi 24, 25, 27—*B xiii 67; C xvi 73.*
xi 26—*B xiii 69; C xvi 75.*

2 Corinthians (*continued*)
 xii 4—*A xii 22*; B *xviii 393*;
  C xxi 440.
 xii 9—*B xvii 335*; *C xx 317*.
Galatians
 i 10—*B xiii 313*; *C vii 60*.
 [ii 11—B xi 87.]
 iii 8—B xvi 247; C xix 267.
 iii 8, 9—B xvi 239; C xix 257.
 iv 4—*B xvi 93*; *C xix 127, 139*.
 vi 2—*B vi 224, xi 205*, cf. C xiii
  117; *C ix 231, xiv 78*.
 vi 5—*B x 112*.
 vi 10—*A xi 238*; B *x 199*.
 vi 14—*B xv 499*; *C xviii 198*.
Ephesians
 iv 8—*B v 498*; *C viii 131*.
 [v 4—A p 38; B p 38; C i 39.]
 [v 25—B xiv 264; C xvii 106.]
 [v 26, 27—A xi 229, cf. B x 346.]
  Quotes passage from S. Mark.
Philippians
 ii 10—B xix *16, 76*; C xxii 16,
  80.
 iii 19—*B ix 60*.
Colossians
 iii 1—*B x 355*.
 [iii 8—A p 38; B p 38; C i 39.]
Thessalonians
 v 15—*C vi 58*.
 v 21—*B iii 335*; *C iv 492, xxi 235*.
1 Timothy
 v 3–14—*C xix 84*.
 [v 20—B xi 87; C xiii 33.]
 [vi 8—B xv 336.]

2 Timothy
 iii 6—*B xx 338*; *C xxiii 340*.
Titus
 [i 13—B xi 87.]
 [ii 15—B xi 87.]
Hebrews
 [x 26, 27—A x 92.]
 x 30—*A xi 247*; *B vi 228, x 204,*
  369.
 [xii 4—B xvi 47.]
S. James
 ii 1—B xv 86; C xvii 240.
 ii 10—*B ix 97, xi 301*; *C xiv 122*.
 ii 26—A i 159; B i 183, *185*; C ii
  182, *184*.
1 S. Peter
 ii 2—*B xi 196*; *C xiii 110*.
 ii 13—*B xi 374*.
 [iii 21—A xi 229, cf. B x 346.]
 iv 18—B xii 278; C xv 203.
 [v 8—B v 186; C vii 168.]
2 S. Peter
 [iii 10—B x 411; C xii 251.]
1 S. John
 [i 9—B xi 81.]
 iii 14—*B xi 170*; *C xiii 98*.
 iv 8—*A i 84*; *B i 86*; *C ii 82*.
 iv 16—*B ix 63*; *C iv 406*.
 iv 18—*B xiii 163*; *C xvi 165*.
Apocalypse
 iii 19—*B xii 12*.
 vi 10—*B xvii 288*; *C xx 270*.
 vii 4–8—B xx 268; C xxiii 269.
 xiv 4, 5—*C xix 84*.
 xiv 13—*B xiv 212*; *C xvii 55*.

INDEX

Italicized references are those of subjects introduced
only in the longer quotations on the page indicated

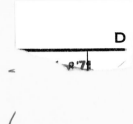

D